WALKS IN THE LAMMERMUIRS

Fast Castle - looking north-west

WALKS IN THE LAMMERMUIRS

Including Moorfoot, Broughton and Culter Hills

by

Alan Hall

CICERONE PRESS
MILNTHORPE, CUMBRIA

Dedicated to My Best Friend

ACKNOWLEDGEMENTS

To tread a path where few have gone before has been a journey of rewarding discovery, made light by the cooperation, encouragement and help of landowners, farmers and shepherds, countryside rangers, rights of way officers, public utilities officials, members of local community councils, local libraries and of course the walking public.

Many thanks to Sheila Pate, Jane Begg, Alan Corson, P. A. Gascoigne, D. F. Harbottle, A. A. Bertram, Malcolm Mackenzie, Drew Jamieson, Neil Clarke, Alex Montgomerie, Douglas Lowe, Hamish Crawford and Mike Baker; your assistance is greatly appreciated.

Also valued were the reminiscences of respected pedestrians, who have delved deeper than I into the mysteries of these Border hills and who dredged their memories for the benefit of the book; my thanks to George McDougall, Bathgate, and Don Struthers, Innerleithen.

Finally my continuing gratitude to Greta who continues to encourage my restless spirit and ageing legs, and to Hector whose eye for a good photograph never dims.

May I acknowledge all who lightened my step and widened my horizons.

All photographs and maps are by the author, and all extracts from poems, couplets etc. carry their authors' name if known.

By the same author:
The Border Country - a walker's guide
Border Pubs & Inns - a walker's guide
Kielder Country Walks
North Pennines - walking guide

Front Cover: Fast Castle

CONTENTS

INTRODUCTION

Background

Action

CHAPTER 1: THE LAMMERMUIR HILLS

CHAPTER 2: THE MOORFOOT HILLS

CHAPTER 3: THE CLOICH HILLS AND THE BROUGHTON HEIGHTS

CHAPTER 4: THE CULTER HILLS

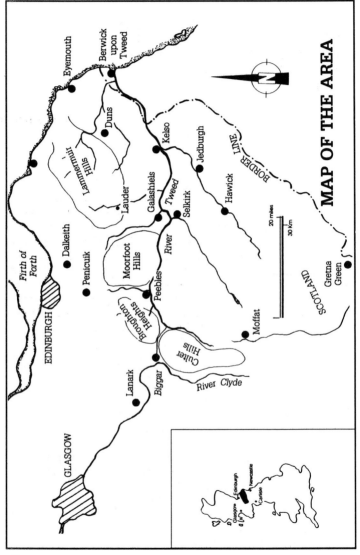

MAP OF THE AREA

THE HILLS OF LAMMERMUIR, MOORFOOT, CLOICH, BROUGHTON AND CULTER

The hills are shadows, and they flow
from form to form, and nothing stands;
They melt like mists, the solid lands,
Like clouds they shape themselves and go.

Robert Eckford

Unknown by many, unwalked by most, these five small ranges form the northern and north-western bastions of the Borderland, a crescent shaped divide separating the Southern Uplands from the rift of the Forth and Clyde valleys. From east to west, sea to source, they run with the Tweed for some 90 miles/144km; never wider than 12 miles/19.2km at any point they nevertheless present formidable barriers to those wishing to leave or enter the Border enclave. Each range is conveniently packaged and separated from its neighbours by deep-gouged south or east flowing watercourses; Gala Water betwixt the Lammermuirs and the Moorfoots, Eddleston Water divides the Moorfoots from the Cloich Hills, which in turn are kept apart from the Broughton Heights by Lyne and Tarth. Finally the Broughton Heights and the Culter Hills are kept at arms length by the east-west divide of the Biggar Gap, through which the undecided flows of Biggar Water pass.

As hills they may lack height and form, the highest Lammermuir being Meikle Says Law, 1755ft/535m. Crowning the Moorfoots is Windlestraw Law, 2162ft/659m, with Culter Fell at 2454ft/748m in the Culter Hills topping them all. Fortunately nature has, as usual, compensated for the diminutive stature of these ranges by peppering them with intriguing highlights, with much to offer the pedestrian.

These solid bastions roll and rise, for all the world like giant mole-hills in a pasture, splashed with purple heather and fringed white by quivering grass; presenting a pleasing and differing aspect of the upland form for those who wish to see, and a stimulating and rewarding challenge for those who wish to walk.

Their outward form has changed much over the last nine millennia since man rambled onto the Border scene. When the ice receded and the earth warmed, the high ground was populated by birch with oak below; home to an extensive spread of wildlife, including wild boar, bear, wolf, elk and red deer. That is until the arrival of our ancestors, when the long slow forest clearances began. First came the trails and tracks, then larger areas were cleared for grazing and crops, later accelerated by the great Cistercian abbeys, which brought not only the word of God to the Borders but also a tradition of sheep farming that has lasted to this day. A factor that has, in conjunction with other geological, biological and economic influences, fashioned our Border hills into the predominantly heather and grass culture of today. Of the five ranges covered in the guide, two, the Moorfoot Hills and the Culter Hills, offer nine mountains and eight tops, from 2000ft/610m to 2499ft/762m - referred to as 'Donalds', from the list compiled by Percy Donald. The highest is Culter Fell at 2454ft/748m. The five ranges of Lammermuir, Moorfoot, Cloich, Broughton and Culter have much in common with their sisters in the Southern Uplands and the Border Hills. For each have their own character, whether that be space and freedom, an eye-catching curve on ridge and corrie, peace and solitude, the finest views in southern Scotland, ease of access, or simply a collection of fine walks. To add interest many of the trails in these hills utilise existing Roman roads, ancient trade routes, monk's 'gaits' and drove roads, enabling today's walker to tread the ways of centurian, cleric, kings, cadgers and cattle. If my enthusiasm for my own backyard has given the impression that all the walks are in the lightweight class do not be misled; there are journeys available that can challenge mind and body alike, yet without subjecting the walker to unwelcome exposure. They simply offer the walker the best of both worlds.

CLIMATE AND WEATHER PATTERNS

The following figures are based on monthly and yearly averages, taken over the period 1970-1989, for the Borders region. They record the weather as it was, and are but an indication, not a forecast, of future weather patterns.

For comparative purposes link the Broughton Heights to the Culter Hills and the Cloich Hills to the Moorfoot Hills.

Sunshine

Hours of Bright Sunshine - Daily Average

Jan	Feb	Mar	Apr	May	Jun	Jul
Lammermuirs - coast						
1.8	2.8	3.7	5.4	6.1	6.7	6.1
Culters - 900ft/275m						
1.3	2.2	2.9	4.5	5.3	5.4	4.6

Aug	Sep	Oct	Nov	Dec	Mean	Annual Total
Lammermuirs - coast						
5.4	4.4	3.4	2.4	4.2	4.2	1523
Culters - 900ft/275m						
4.3	3.3	2.5	1.8	1.2	3.3	1198

The combination of distance from the coast and height above sea level has a definite bearing on the hours of sunshine, with the eastern coastal Lammermuirs likely to enjoy 45-50% more sunshine than the western flanks of the Culter Hills. The ranges running west to east from the Culters benefit proportionately the further east they are, just as the eastern fringes of each range are likely to have more sunshine than the western flanks.

Temperature

Daily Average at Lammermuir coast, degrees Celsius

	Maximum	Minimum
January	5.8°	0°
July	19.4°	10.6°

As height above sea level is gained so does the temperature decline, as a simple Lapse Rate calculation will show; a reduction of 3°C for every 1000ft/305m increase in height above sea level. For winter walks cold air also drains into the valley floors forming frost pockets, thus making the entire journey a chilling experience.

Visibility

The hills in question sit in one of the least populated and least industrialised areas of the UK, and as such enjoy all the benefits that accrue, with many days of clear air and distant vistas. With no industrial or traffic pollution, water-based night fogs, should they occur, quickly disperse with the morning sun. Sea Haars, during the months from April to September, do sometimes blight the Berwickshire coast where the Lammermuirs tumble into the sea.

Wind

The entire Border region lies within a prevailing south-west air flow, with winds blowing in from that particular quadrant twice as frequently as from any other point of the compass. The hill ranges covered in this guide, situated as they are on the eastern half of the country, enjoy calm conditions for the majority of the year. Five per cent of the time speeds are below 1 mile / 1.6km per hour and 85% of the year wind speeds keep within the bracket $1^{1}/_{2}$-$18^{1}/_{2}$ miles / 2.4-29.6km per hour. However recent winters have experienced an increase in wind speeds, with gusts exceeding 60 miles / 96km per hour, which are but mere zephyrs compared with the roaring gales frequently experienced in their opposite corner of Scotland. The calmest period in which to enjoy the ranges running west from the coast to the Culter Hills is April to October, whilst December to March produces savage winds of a thin nature from the north. On such occasions it is wise to avoid the northern flanks and summits, of all ranges, as the Firth of Forth and the Lothian plains give little comfort or shelter.

Precipitation

Annual Rainfall - inches

	Heights	Valleys	Driest Months	Wettest Months
Lammermuirs	34.51	26.35	Mar Apr Jun	Aug Nov Jan
Moorfoots	39.90	34.60	Mar Jun Apr	Aug Nov Dec/Jan
Culters	55.00	38.00	Jun Mar Apr	Nov Dec Aug

Average Rainfall - inches per month

	Driest Months	*Wettest Months*
Lammermuirs	1.80	3.16
Moorfoots	2.46	3.78
Culters	2.93	4.82

The prevailing south-westerly winds, having gathered moisture from the Atlantic Ocean, will naturally deposit the bulk of their rain on the most westerly of the ranges and on the most westerly flanks of each range, as can be seen from the above tables. All the Border's upland areas have a relatively low rainfall when compared with the highlands of the west coast; indeed I would hazard a guess that the Lammermuir Hills enjoy drier conditions overhead than any other range in Britain above 1500ft/457m.

The incidence of summer thunderstorms and hail showers in the Borders is also low, appearing on average no more than seven times per year.

Snow
Days per Month with Lying Snow at 0900hrs

Altitude	*Jan*	*Feb*	*Mar*	*Apr*	*May*	*Jun*
1000ft	9.5	9	4.5	0.5	0	0
	Jul	*Aug*	*Sep*	*Oct*	*Nov*	*Dec*
	0	0	0	0	2	5

Rarely does a covering of snow prevent access to, or progress over, even the highest mountain in each range, thus allowing the walker to enjoy these hills under a different cloak.

When to Walk
The above figures and long experience suggest that June is the prime time to walk these northern Border bastions; long, bright and dry days with little or no wind, in temperatures to suit at any level. April, May and July, with only small variations in overhead conditions, are in close pursuit, although it can be said that any time is a good time to walk the Border hills.

FLORA AND FAUNA

Flora

All the ranges are well furnished with the usual Southern Upland species. Heather (*calluna*) is dominant on the dry slopes and plateaux, particularly on the Broughton Heights and the Lammermuir Hills, on whose drier eastern slopes bell heather (*erica cinerea*) also flourishes. On the more moist soils and peaty plateaux to the west the most prominant and widespread is bog heather (*erica tetralix*). Blaeberry is also frequent and dominant on some summits, along with cowberry and cloudberry. It is of interest that cloudberry can only be found in one place in the Lammermuir Hills, high on the southern flank of Fallago Ridge above the source of Dye Water. The large green leaves and white or rose flowers bear the orange-red fruit sporadically - could this be due to the lack of height in the Lammermuirs, for seldom in the Border hills have I found cloudberry growing below 1700ft/518m? Three mosses of the club moss family, in company with the ubiquitous sphagnum, are ever present on our high hills, thriving in the wet areas. Learn to recognize your heathers and mosses as both are useful guides in warning the walker of dry/wet conditions underfoot.

Indigenous grasses flourish at all levels. The most extensive ground cover in the Southern Uplands, they provide a hallmark for these distinctive hills. Tussocks of purple moor grass, patches of cotton grass (thrives in wet conditions) and upland prairies of matgrass and wavy hair grass on the tops and high plateaux inform the walker that s/he is in the Border hills. At lower levels bents, fescues and Yorkshire fog grow, with patches of rushes crowding the wet holes and burnsides. Competition on our hillsides, for nutrients and light, is severe and it appears that the grasses are losing out to the spread of the insidious bracken, at the rate of up to 10% per year.

Trees, once the most prevalent ground cover in the area, that is before the hand of man and the ubiquitous sheep cleared the land, are staging a comeback. Sadly for the ascetic this resurgence of the tree is in the form of geometrical coniferous monocultures that scar the fells, and if in great profusion, increase local precipitation. Such areas of spruce can be found in the eastern Lammermuirs, extensively on the south-west Moorfoots and the Cloich Hills, the northern and eastern flanks of the Broughton Heights, with one or two blotches on the south-eastern fringes and the lower central fells of the Culter Hills. Happily, the more enlightened foresters are now restructuring and landscaping the larger forests with broadleaves, in addition to welcoming outdoor enthusiasts. Natural regeneration of such sylvan delights as oak, ash, beech, sycamore, rowan, silver birch, alder and hazel only occurs at lower levels by riverbanks and lochsides, or at burnsides and sheltered cleuchs at higher elevations.

The eastern cliffs and coastline where the Lammermuirs tumble dramatically into the North Sea are home to a carpet of sea pink, mouse eared chickweed, rock rose and sheep's fescue, with many meadow plants growing on the sides of nearby lochs and lochans.

Fauna
Birds
It will come as no surprise to the ornithologist that in excess of 300 different birds inhabit the border areas covered in this guide. Many, such as the familiar blackbird, heron, robin, rook, pigeon, grouse, partridge, owl, kestrel, gull and guillemot stay with us all year. With the approach of the cold weather in autumn many of the more colourful characters leave for warmer climes to return in the spring; birds such as the plover, swallow, swift, ring ouzel and cuckoo. Thankfully these migrants are replaced by other hardier souls, who consider the borders a suitable place to winter, flying in from the north; species such as fieldfares, snow bunting, pink-geese and grey lags. Then there are those birds of passage who rest awhile in the borders, either in transit south in autumn, or north in spring - the missel thrush, dotterel and osprey. Not forgetting the common curlew, or whaup as it is known in these parts, beloved by the hill walker, who spends summer on the high and windswept fells, and winter by the seashore.

Raptors, many of whom departed from this area due to lack of food supplies and the guns and poisons of the Victorian 'keepers, have now returned, with every species ever recorded in the borders now re-established.

The largest colony of nesting seabirds in south-east Scotland screech and wheel by the towering cliffs of the coastal Lammermuirs: fulmers, herring gulls, shags, guillemots, puffins and razor bills. So many species of birds grace our seashore and cliffs, valleys and waterways, lochans and mires, fells and cleuchs, ridges and mountains. There is always a bird to please the eye and the ear, to add interest to the journey and to lighten the step.

Mammals
Sadly, conservation did not carry a high rating on our ancestors' list of priorities, thus many of the mammals, in particular the larger and tastier ones, no longer roam the border fells and wilderness areas. Due entirely to man's heavy hand we have lost forever bear, wolf, ox, elk, beaver, wild boar and red deer from our uplands.

At higher levels feral goats roam in small herds, the availability of food keeping the numbers to around twenty; also the fox can be found, as can the bounding mountain hare with its distinctive white winter coat. By burnside and lochans frogs, toads, slow-worm, newts, and now the escaped feral mink abound, who, in addition to stoats and weasels, have an appetite for the tasty fieldmouse and vole. Snakes are present in the shape of the shy adder, distinct with its dark zigzag back markings, which will invariably slither into the undergrowth when disturbed. Should this venomous, though not poisonous, snake bite you it is indeed advisable to seek immediate qualified medical attention.

HISTORY AND GEOLOGY
Physical History
Contrary to the general appearance of the Border hills, that is, of endless folds of rounded hills and flowing ridges suggesting an orderly, mainly horizontal, deposit of base rock as the earth was formed, what in truth actually happened was as violent and cataclysmic an eruption as was man's progress through the ages of Border life.

The basic rock of the Southern Uplands, mainly Ordovician and Silurian, is of great age with a highly complex geological structure which has, through the course of time and with unimaginable force, been pressed into a series of isoclinal folds. Basically in a north-east and south-west direction, they have in some cases had the axes tilted north-west and south-east, causing the older strata (originally up to 20,000ft/6,096m thick) to overlie the newer strata. A trauma that caused the Border skyline to resemble more the Dolomites than the hills we see today.

Three geographical belts lie parallel to the main folds. The Northern Belt contains the northern Lammermuirs, the Moorfoots and the Broughton Heights and comprises mainly Ordovician strata. The Central Belt embrace the Culter Hills east to the Moffat Hills, Melrose and the coast at St Abbs and is made up chiefly of Silurian strata with splashes of Ordovician folds. This belt also exhibits the deposits of the Silurian Age, separated by a line running south-west from the Moorfoots at Innerleithen via what is now the Tweed to Kingledoors Burn in the Culters. The Southern Belt is outwith the area of this guide.

Through the ravages of incomprehensible time and irresistible elements thousands of feet of strata have been ripped off and transported to the sea, stripping the mountains of their former grandeur and leaving only the stumps we see today. The rocks, directly beneath the walker's boot, are therefore mainly sedimentary, shales, cherts, grits, mudstones, greywacke, limestones, sandstones and conglomerates, that have in parts been penetrated and interleaved with igneous (*resulting from fire*) rocks. Interestingly the oldest rocks in the area, the Arenig Lavas, can be seen in a narrow surface belt running south-west through the Broughton Heights near Riddenlees.

Another feature of the geological picture in the area is the presence of Dykes, intrusions of molten material from the earth's interior into cracks and fissures in the earth's crust and lying in the same direction as the sedimentary rocks. Examples of these can be found in the Moorfoots, at Kirnie Hill, Priesthope and the famed mineral spring at St Ronans Wells, with a vein of minerals lying on the base granite.

The Tweed and its Tributaries
A theory has been advanced that in Tertiary times the Tweed flowed from the hills of Dumbartonshire, following the course of today's lower Clyde, then passed through the Biggar Gap into upper Tweeddale, a theory supported by the relative size of the Biggar Gap. Then came the Pliocene upheavals, elevating the land in the west and north-west whilst gently sloping (relatively speaking)

the land to the east and south-east, which in effect closed the Biggar Gap and reversed the flow of the Clyde. Now fed from Tweeds Well, today's Tweed flanks the Culter Hills to Drumelzier, a distance of some 13 miles/20.5km in which it falls 45ft/14m per mile/1.6km. For the next 24 miles/38.4km it falls a mere 14ft/4.25m per mile, suggesting that perhaps the present surging flow in the upper reaches was at one time a mere tributary of the original mightier Tweed.

The Ice Age

Two major ice invasions finally fashioned the Southern Uplands.

1) A massive ice sheet of great thickness covered even the highest peaks, and as it was independent of the drainage lines it tended to move in the general direction of the Tweed depression. Drumlins show an east-south-east movement, resulting in a smoothing and rounding of the hills on their western flanks; whilst the leeward sides remained relatively protected. Note today's jagged exposed rock, crags and scree, examples of which can be seen in all the ranges covered in the guide, especially Lee Pen and Pirn Craig in the Moorfoots.

2) A period of high glacier activity, when all but the highest summits were covered, resulted in the abrasion of encroaching ridges, producing severed spurs. Such friction tended also to straighten the valley, evidence of which can be seen at the steep face at Cadon Bank, Innerleithen.

As the ice melted and retreated north it left behind a changed landscape. Phenomena such as Kames and Eskers, glacial debris from meltwater deposited in ridges and terraces, can be seen at The Kames on Greenlaw Moor in the Lammermuirs. Meltwater channels also give the Lammermuirs a unique character, perhaps in the eyes of Lammerphiles their greatest asset. Clay deposits also clothed the hills allowing, through time, vegetation to grow and spread, the idiograph of today's Southern Uplands.

Minerals

The mining of minerals has, at one time, occurred in all the ranges covered in the guide. Limestone of the Caradoc age was mined at Wrae Hill on the Culter fringes in 1795, slate was quarried at Stobo by the Broughton Heights, and blue and grey greywacke was taken from the Moorfoots to construct houses in Innerleithen.

Human History

> *There came a man, by middle day,*
> *He spied his sport and went away;*
> *And brought the King that very night,*
> *Who brake my bower and slew my knight.*

Anon

Serious human intrusion into the fringes of the Southern Uplands, by penetration along the banks of watercourses north and west of the Tweed, began in and around 6000 BC in what is known as the Mesolithic period or early Stone Age. Woodlands were cleared and crops were grown, thus beginning the long process of deforestation. When Neolithic man arrived around 3500 BC with his 'advanced' agricultural techniques denudation was accelerated; as was the building of collective burial places, eg. the long cairn known as the Mutiny Stones above Dye Water in the Lammermuirs. Bronze Age man in 2000 BC moved up in the world, due no doubt to an increasingly warm and dry climate, the undrained valley floor and the need to protect himself on higher ground. Evidence of his forts, settlements with cairns and cists, stone circles and standing stones remain today and can be seen by the observant walker on the majority of hill ranges (mentioned in the individual walks). From 1000 BC Iron Age technology added pallisaded forts, settlements, and a developing arable and livestock farming to the area, prime examples being Dreva Craig in the Broughton Heights and a whole crop on the north-eastern flanks of Lauderdale, perched on truncated spurs between the 1000 and 1250ft/305 & 381m contour.

From AD 80 to 400 the Southern Uplands and the Lothian plain were occupied, and to a great extent administered, by the Legions of Rome. Such was the Roman character, the wilder the country the more roads were built, and so it was in the Borders. The principal route was Dere Street running north from Trimontium, Melrose through Lauderdale, then over the Lammermuirs at Soutra to Inveresk, with a camp at Channelkirk. Well Path, another major thoroughfare, also ran north via a camp at Crawford in the upper Clyde Valley, skirting the Culter Hills and clipping the Broughton Heights, making a bee-line north-east also to Inveresk - at the mouth of the Esk. This road was connected to a strategically placed major camp at Lyne on the confluence of Lyne Water and the River Tweed.

The major Celtic tribes, the Selgovae in the Moorfoots and Broughton Heights and the Ottadini or Votadini in the Lammermuirs, are believed, to a greater extent, to have accepted Roman domination. Their forts and settlements were intact and often in the vicinity of Roman camps. After the Roman withdrawal, around AD 400, tribal life settled down to its traditional border ways, with rival Celtic tribes soon at each other's throats; that is when they were not fending off attacks from the Scots and Picts from the north and Angles from the south; a way of life that was to smoulder, and often flame, throughout the Borders for nigh on 1100 years. Celtic communities from Clydeside and Northumbria did however bring Christianity to this battlefield, which was followed in the 12th century by an outburst of ecclesiastical building, witness the many fine Border abbeys and priories.

Trade and agriculture, particularly sheep, flourished in medieval times, surprisingly, for during the period from 1124 to 1603 the Borders was trampled underfoot by the armies of Scotland and England as they ebbed and flowed over the rolling Border hills. And when the swath was cut and the booty harvested, the local reivers - Fighting Families - were back to settling feuds and stealing stock. Yet in this time of strife many paths and 'rodes', such as Dere Street by the military, Girthgate by pilgrims, the Herring Road by fish-cadgers and the Thief's Road by reivers, were laid down over ridge and fell, by cleuch and lochside, and are still available for today's pedestrian.

With the Union of the Crowns in 1603 came a slow and tedious hundred-year period of pacification, before peace and prosperity finally gained the upper hand. And even today by many a cleuch and lonely fell, whether in the Lammermuirs or on the Moorfoots, the voices and sounds of that violent past come whispering by on the sighing wind.

The old ways and tracks, together with the relics of yesteryear, are detailed in the appropriate walks description throughout the guide.

RIGHTS OF WAY AND PUBLIC PATHS

This is a grey and troubled area, and it is not within the remit of this guide to go further than state the four criteria needed to establish and maintain a public right of way.

1. It must have been used by the general public for a continuous period of twenty years.
2. It must have been used as a matter of right.
3. It must connect two public places.
4. It must follow a route more or less defined.

Two publications are recommended: *A Walker's Guide to the Rights of Way in Scotland,* Scottish Rights of Way Society Ltd, John Cotton Business Centre, 10/2 Sunnyside, Edinburgh EH7 5RA; and *Public Rights of Way in the Borders Region,* Planning Department, Scottish Borders Council, Newtown St Boswells, Melrose TD6 0SA. For rights of way details concerning specific paths contact the addresses above.

Unlike England, the hills of Scotland, and in particular the Southern Uplands, are practically void of rights of way paths and waymarked ways. This does not mean that paths and tracks do not exist. They do and have done for generations, even though they are not marked on the OS maps, thanks to understanding and goodwill between estate owners and hill walkers regarding access to Border hills. Such routes, hallowed by custom and tradition, are a privilege, not a right and should be treated accordingly; nor does inclusion in the guide imply a right of way.

Whilst every effort has been made by the author, in checking the feasibility and accessibility of the included walks, circumstances and ownership may change, affecting passage. Objections are rare providing the Country Code is observed, although a trend of restricted access is showing itself on certain holdings in recent years, invariably on estates with a new laird, who is unfamiliar with the practices of our countryside. In such cases polite common sense repeatedly prevails.

The law of trespass differs in Scotland and England and this guide is not qualified to lead the walker through either minefield. The author has found that a serious and courteous enquiry to the landowner, farmer or shepherd regarding the feasibility of a certain route makes life so much easier for all concerned. To show concern for others' property, as well as the environment, is to show concern for the entire countryside.

ACCESS AND ACCOMMODATION

Access

Rail Links

Two main lines clip the eastern and western fringes of the ranges covered in the guide, stopping at Berwick-upon-Tweed and Edinburgh on the east coast intercity line, and Carlisle and Lockerbie on the west coast intercity link. (Carlisle station is connected to the Borders by the Scottish Borders Rail Link bus.)

Frequent intercity services stop at Edinburgh and Berwick-upon-Tweed each day, with several slower stopping trains supplementing this service. Lockerbie and Carlisle are served from Glasgow, the west of England, Wales and London. Timetables, tickets and fare details are available from Scotrail and British Rail stations, plus British Rail Travel Agents offices. The telephone numbers of the four stations serving the area are given under Useful Addresses and Telephone Numbers.

Road Links

By car from the eastern half of England, the A1, M1, and A1M roads lead north to Tyneside, and from there the A1 continues north to Berwick-upon-Tweed. Scenic routes from Newcastle-upon-Tyne are the A697 road to Coldstream and Greenlaw (Lammermuirs), and the A68(T) road directly crossing the Border to Lauder (Lammermuirs). Branch from the A68(T) at Newtown St Boswells to Galashiels, from where the A72 leads to Peebles (Moorfoots, Cloich Hills, Broughton Heights and Culter Hills). For southbound travellers five roads lead from Edinburgh direct to the ranges covered in this guide: the A701 to Moffat (Cloich Hills, Broughton Heights and Culter Fells), the A703 to Peebles (Cloich Hills, Moorfoots), the A7 to Galashiels (Moorfoots), the A68(T) to Lauder (Lammermuirs), and the A1(T) to Berwick-upon-Tweed (Lammermuirs).

To reach the Southern Uplands from the south-west of England and Wales use the M6 north to Carlisle, then travel (a) north-east on the A7 Borders scenic route to Galashiels (Moorfoots) and on to

Peebles via the A72 (Cloich Hills) or to Lauder via the A68 (Lammermuirs), or (b) on the A74(T) to Crawford (Culter Hills) or to Moffat, then via the A701 for Edinburgh (Culter Hills, Broughton Heights and Cloich Hills). From Glasgow use the M74 and A74 to Crawford (Culter Hills), the A72 to Biggar (Culter Hills), the A721 to Blyth Bridge (Broughton Heights and Cloich Hills) or continue with the A72 to Peebles and Galashiels (Moorfoots and Lammermuirs).

When a walker's car to the start of a walk is used and parking space is limited, care and consideration should be exercised, to ensure access and passage are not restricted for those who live and work in the area.

Bus Services
Long distance express bus services from many major cities and towns (including four airports) in England and Scotland pass through the Borders and Southern Uplands, stopping at Galashiels and Jedburgh. Western fringes of the area are served by long distance buses from the west of Scotland, England and Wales, calling at Carlisle, Moffat and Biggar.

Local Services
As in the majority of wild and lonely areas, the Southern Uplands are not particularly well served by local bus services. School buses can be used in some areas, as can the Post Bus (remember many of the remote areas have only one delivery/collection per day). To supplement these services from July to September (inclusive) the Harrier Bus is routed to call at the tourist parts other buses do not reach. The majority of walks in the guide can be reached by a local bus service of one type or another, though not always at times to suit the walker, nor can the return trip be guaranteed. Bus guides are available from bus offices, the Scottish Borders tourist information offices, Scottish Borders Council, Edinburgh and Lothian tourist offices plus Clyde Valley tourist offices; contacts are detailed under Useful Information.

Accommodation
The walks are arranged in groups with one base covering several

walks, thus reducing the need to be continually hunting for overnight accommodation. A wide and varied selection of accommodation is available in the area to suit all tastes and pockets. To assist the walker as to the most convenient place to stay, all walks descriptions list the nearest township/village providing accommodation.

Accommodation details and booking arrangements are obtained from tourist information centres and youth hostels, details of which are given under Useful Information.

THE GUIDE
Aims
The aim is to produce a comprehensive walks guide that is as comfortable and easy to understand as it is to carry, a guide that is graphically accurate and verbally stimulating. All routes in the guide have been walked by the author several times, and a few special favourites many times. The journeys have been planned to suit all tastes, whether of the enthusiastic hill walker or the relaxed valley stroller.

Layout
The area is divided into Chapters, 1 to 4, each one self-contained and geographically different from its fellows. The more mountainous and hilly sections contain a higher proportion of hill walks, such as those in Chapters 2 and 4, whilst the walks in Chapters 1 and 3 are of an easier and more gentle nature.

Sixteen walks in the Lammermuir Hills, a neglected moorland plateau with some intriguing watercourses, are included in Chapter 1. Chapter 2, with fifteen walks, traverses the domes and ridges of the Moorfoot Hills high above picturesque Tweeddale and the Lothian plain. Chapter 3 includes ten walks in the more gentle and winsome uplands of the Cloich Hills and the fine of form Broughton Heights. Chapter 4 treads the lonely tops and glistening reservoir shores of the Culter Hills with nine, often demanding, walks.

Several long and demanding routes are scattered throughout the chapters, such as the Herring Road, Dundreich-Lee Pen Ridgeway and Bagging Thirteen Broughtons. Such walks demand respect and should only be undertaken by fit and experienced hill walkers who require that little bit extra from the Southern Uplands and Border hills.

An Information Table follows, including items of specific interest linked to various walks, for easy and quick reference. A Glossary of local names and dialect words relating to the area is followed by the Bibliography, and finally, lists of Addresses for accommodation, transport, various organisations and weather forecasts.

Walk details

Each chapter introduces the specific range with a landscape portrait, plus a simple map showing the numbered location of each walk. This is followed by a thumb-nail description of the numbered walks, together with details of relevant maps, and an Information Table detailing Distance, Height Gain, Degree of Difficulty and Time Required, for instant and easy reference. All walks are graded, from 1 to 4, with a Degree of Difficulty classification (1 being the shorter and easier walk, 4 being long and demanding). The D of D gradings are included in all the Information Tables, together with a full explanation of the classification.

Each walk is then described in detail, with an easy-to-read map showing the suggested route, and a blow-by-blow account of the journey (with 6-figure map references and compass bearings if necessary). Instructions to turn left or right are invariably accompanied by the clarification "ie. east or west".

The picture is finally completed by Items of Interest Along the Way. Each item is numbered and keyed, for clarity, into the text of the route description, eg. Gypsy's Blood (5) or Dundreich (1), thus leaving the route description continuous, uncluttered and easy to follow. The Items of Interest can then be perused at the walker's leisure.

Walks are timed using the tried and tested formulae of W W Naismith. For each 3 miles (4.8km) of linear distance allow 1 hour, and should an ascent be made in that distance add 30 minutes to the walking time for each 1000ft (305m) of ascent. The resultant times calculated using the Naismith formula have been tempered by the author's own timings, depending on the terrain, the weather conditions, and the frequency of refreshment, photographic, breath replacement and convenience stops. It is not the intention of this guide to include endurance tests.

SPECIAL INTERESTS TABLE

Interest	Chapter	Walk
ANTIQUITY	1	1, 2, 3, 8, 9, 10, 11
	2	9, 11, 14
	3	1, 2, 4, 6, 8
	4	4
DROVE ROADS	1	3, 4, 5, 6, 8, 9, 10, 11
	2	1
	3	1, 2, 3, 5, 9
	4	4
ECCLESIASTICAL	1	4, 5, 8, 11
	2	10, 13, 14
	3	1, 2, 3, 5, 8, 9
	4	9
FLORA & FAUNA	1	1, 2, 3, 6, 7, 8, 9, 12
	2	1, 2-4, 5-8, 9,11, 12, 13, 14
	3	1, 2, 3, 6, 7, 8, 9, 10
	4	1, 2, 3, 4, 6, 7, 8, 9
GEOLOGY	1	1, 9, 10
	2	4, 9, 10, 11, 12, 14
	3	5, 6, 8
	4	1, 3, 4, 5, 6, 8
HISTORICAL	1	1, 2, 4, 5, 6, 8, 9, 10, 11
	2	1, 2, 3, 4, 10, 11, 12, 13, 14
	3	1, 2, 3, 6, 7, 8, 9
	4	1, 3, 4, 7
LITERARY	1	4, 10
	2	1, 4
	3	6
	4	7
OLD INDUSTRY	1	10, 11
	2	10, 11, 13
	3	2, 3, 8
	4	3, 4, 7

Interest	Chapter	Walk
PHOTOGRAPHY	1	1, 2, 5, 6, 7, 9, 10, 11
	2	4, 8, 10, 11, 12, 13, 14
	3	3, 5, 6, 7, 8
	4	1, 3, 4, 6, 9
SCENIC BEAUTY	1	1, 2, 3, 4, 5, 7, 8, 9, 11
	2	4, 8, 9, 10, 11, 12, 13, 14
	3	3, 4, 6, 7, 8, 10
	4	1, 2, 3, 4, 5, 6, 8, 9
WALKS - CHALLENGING	1	1, 8, 9, 11
	2	9, 10, 11, 12, 13, 14
	3	7, 8, 10
	4	1, 2, 3, 5, 6, 8, 9
WALKS - GENTLE	1	7
	2	2, 3
	3	5, 9
	4	4, 7
WATERCOURSES	1	2, 3, 5, 7, 8, 9, 11
	2	1, 4, 10, 13, 14
	3	3, 5, 8, 9
	4	3, 4, 5, 7, 9

CLOTHING AND EQUIPMENT

The vexed question of what to wear and what to take on a walk is solved by four words: CONDITIONS DETERMINE CLOTHING/EQUIPMENT. It matters not whether that walk is a stroll on a balmy summer evening, or a mountain hike on a stormy February day, the answer is always the same. Conditions underfoot and overhead will determine clothing and footwear.

Conditions Underfoot
What to Expect on the Southern Uplands

The Lammermuirs, Moorfoots, Cloich Hills, Broughton Heights and Culter Hills, at levels below 1500ft/458m, are traversed either by farm/cart tracks or grass covered paths, and invariably provide good dry walking. Above 1500ft conditions vary a great deal, from narrow dry traces over short and springy grass (as found on the summits of Windlestraw Law, Dundreich and Culter Fell), to teazled blankets of deep heather (as experienced on most of the Lammermuir plateau, the upper Moorfoots, the Broughton Heights and Culter Hills), with fortunately few areas of extensive peat hags (the exceptions being Blackhope Scar and Garvald Punks - Moorfoots, and King Bank Head - Culters). Avoid patches of bright green moss such as sphagnum or featherbed moss, which invariably grow over wet-holes. Cotton grass and rushes also signal water underfoot and should be given a wide berth if possible. Bilberry, bents and molina grass on the other hand signal dry paths, so choose your footwear accordingly.

Choose lightweight boots or well soled trainers for the lower levels, middle weight leather boots for the higher levels and rigid soled leather boots for the few rock/boulder traverses that are encountered. Footwear chosen wisely will shorten the journey; take the wrong option and the walk could be a disaster. Be comfortable.

Conditions Overhead
What to Expect on the Southern Uplands

The area, situated as it is on the eastern side of the country, does not experience the precipitation excesses experienced in other places. Nor does it suffer from the searing winds encountered above 3000ft/915m, for the ranges in question do not exceed 2500ft/762m, although an occasional evil north-easter can bring tears to the walker's eyes. Hours of sunshine also exceed the national average, but due to the latitude temperatures never become unbearable. Choose clothes to keep you warm and dry in winter and cool in summer, loose fitting garments made of natural fibres, plus a hat to protect against the sun's rays.

Temperature and moisture are of great importance to the hill walker. If both are in balance and agreeable to the pedestrian then the walk will be a pleasure. If not and the walker is ill-prepared, they are unwisely exposing themselves to the twin risks of hyperthermia and dehydration/heat exhaustion. Hyperthermia can strike if the temperature of the body core drops below 98.4°F in continuous cold and wet conditions. Dehydration or heat exhaustion can be induced by exposing the body, and in particular the head, to excess heat coupled with an inadequate liquid intake. Carry a filled water bottle.

In winter there is always the threat of the Wind Chill Factor - an increase of 10 miles/16km per hour in wind speed can reduce the temperature from 18°C to 7°C, or in colder conditions from 10°C to -13°C. Also bear in mind the Lapse Rate - the higher the climb the lower the temperature; for every 1000ft/305m ascended there is a reduction of approximately 3°C.

Experienced and committed footsloggers also have been known to carry that little something to ward off vicious elemental spirits. For those not yet into the mystique of what's in the walker's sack, apart from the *de rigeur* bin-liner, let me list the essentials for the Southern Uplands.

High Level
A windproof and waterproof anorak/cagoule, waterproof overtrousers or gaiters, a woolly hat (cotton in the summer), woollen gloves/mitts and a survival bag. High-energy food with a hot drink in winter/large water filled bottle in summer, and for long walks emergency rations such as dried fruit, chocolate, Kendal mint cake, or best of all, homemade rich fruit cake.

Low Level
Walking in summer at the lower levels, particularly in the sheltered valleys, can induce heat exhaustion/dehydration if the walker is unprotected and exposed for long periods. A lightweight cotton hat with a floppy brim, and a full water bottle, will provide all the protection needed. The heated discussions concerning shorts versus long trousers are best settled, as we started, by four words - SCRATCHED LEGS/WHITE LEGS? This guidebook should also be carried at all times.

SAFETY
Whilst all the walks in the guide are designed primarily for the walker's pleasure, safety in the great outdoors is something we must all be aware of. A careless step into a rabbit scrape or on a loose stone could cause a major problem for the solitary walker. It is prudent to be familiar with emergency procedures, and the

equipment needed to minimise discomfort and aid rescue should such an accident occur.

Equipment

1. First-aid kit, including basic dressings, zinc tape, crepe / elasticated bandages (tubi-grip), antiseptic cream, scissors / knife and salt tablets. Any medication carried must only be for personal use, as it is unwise and risky to administer painkillers / drugs to another unless medically qualified.

2. A basic knowledge of First aid should be carried in the head or in the sack.

3. A knife, torch (with spare batteries and bulb), whistle, spare laces (double up as binding), emergency high-energy rations and water, survival bag, compass and map, paper and pen / pencil.

Action

1. Prevention is always advocated: "Heed well the placement of the Feet".

2. Solitude in the hills is prized and much sought after, though for safety's sake three to five walkers, of a like mind and ability, is an ideal number. Such an ideal is not always possible, therefore to reduce the risks observe a few simple guidelines and use that under-employed asset, common sense.

3. Always inform someone of your route and ETR (estimated time of return). If that is not possible leave details of your route plan, number in the party and colour of garments in a visible position in your car. Although in some areas this may be an invitation to the car thief, cars can however be replaced, human life cannot.

4. Should you have the misfortune to be immobilised and require help use the international rescue call - six long blasts on a whistle, or flashes with a torch, repeated at one-minute intervals. The reply is three short blasts at minute intervals. Should you be without whistle or torch, SHOUT using the same code. When waiting for help, use the terrain to gain protection from the elements. Shelter from wind and rain / snow, or the sun in summer, and utilise spare clothing and the survival bag (feet pointing to the wind) to maintain body temperature.

5. Should an accident occur when with companions, write your position on paper (a six-figure map reference - Eastings first, ie. the immediate vertical grid line to the left of your position, then the number of tenths from the grid line to your position, then Northings, repeating the procedure using the horizontal grid line below the position - as instructed on the OS map). Include the name, injury and time sustained, general health, age and clothing, and dispatch an able-bodied member to the nearest telephone (farmhouse etc, or public telephone as indicated on the OS map). At the phone dial 999 (police), who co-ordinate the local rescue teams and rescue operations. When the Mountain Rescue Team is requested, the victim MUST STAY PUT until help arrives.

COUNTRY CODE

Respect the countryside and all that lives and grows therein, and at all times endeavour to leave it in a better state than you found it.

1. Guard against all risk of fire.
2. Fasten all gates.
3. Keep all dogs under complete control. *Do not take dogs on the open fell during nesting time or lambing time.*
4. Use stiles and gates to cross fences and stone dykes.
5. Keep to public rights of way, bridlepaths and footpaths, and do not step onto crops on farmland.
6. Leave livestock, crops and farm machinery alone, no matter how appealing or interesting they may look.
7. If you can carry a Mars bar to the summit of a mountain, you can carry the wrapper back. Take your litter home.
8. Do not pollute any water supplies.
9. Do not disturb or damage wildlife, plants or trees.
10. Respect others' property and privacy; treat it as you would have others treat yours.
11. Prejudices should be left at home.

The uplands covered in this guide are predominantly sheep and grouse country, as your eyes and ears, as well as your choked cleats, will tell you. Respect the property of those who live and work on these hills, keep to the paths during lambing and nesting, and avoid the grouse moors from August 12th to December 10th.

MAPS LEGEND

→	START OF WALK
	BOUNDARY
	VILLAGE OR TOWNSHIP
	FARM BUILDINGS OR HOUSE
	ROAD SUITABLE FOR MOTORISED VEHICLE
	FARM, FOREST OR CART TRACK
	ROUTE/FOOTPATH WITH DIRECTION
	RAILWAY
	LOCH/RESERVOIR
	RIVER/WATER
	BURN/STREAM
	BRIDGE
	CLIFFS
	SUMMIT OF MOUNTAIN OR HILL & LEADING RIDGE
	HIGH EXPOSURE, CRAG, CLIFF OR SCREE
	CAIRN
	PREHISTORIC FORT, SETTLEMENT OR CULTIVATION TERRACES
	ABBEY, MONASTERY OR CHURCH
	CASTLE OR PELE TOWER
	TOWER
	FOREST OR PLANTATION (BROAD LEAVED/ CONIFERS)
	FOREST BOUNDARY
	NATIONAL GRID PYLONS

Fast Castle (Ch.1. Walk 1)

Whiteadder Water reservoir and Killpallet Rig (Ch.1. Walk 5)

Crib Law - heather burn (Ch.1. Walk 9)
Soutra Aisle and patient (Ch.1. Walk 10)

CHAPTER 1
Lammermuir Hills

I love to see the purple bloom across the moorland spread,
The purple bloom o' Lammermuir, I love, I love to tread;
I love to wander by the marsh that plough has never torn,
I love to see the reed tufts wave where ne'er has waved the corn.
Dr Henderson

THE AREA

The Lammermuir (Scots, *Lammer* - Amber, *Muir* - Moor) Hills, an unbroken barrier guarding the north-eastern reaches of the Borders, have also been described, incorrectly in my view, as "wild, cheerless unsightly heights". Also recorded in 1547 was a lament to the banks of Pease Burn, "that who goeth straight doune salbe in daunger of tumbling, and the cummer up so, sure of puffing and payne: for remedie whereof, travailers that have used to pas it, not by going directly, but by paths and foot ways leading slopewise, of the number of which paths, they call it (somewhat nicely in dede) Ye Peaths".

An upland range, with no pretentions of form or grandeur, regarded by some as the unadventurous ugly duckling of the Border hills. Yet, as in all matters pedestrian, there is beauty, solitude, challenge and reward to be found by those who explore the many hidden recesses of the emerging swan. May I, with the aid of this guide, lead the walker away from 'Ye Peaths' onto 'The Paths' and assist you to the Lammermuirs of Dr Henderson.

Originally an offshoot of much higher mountains, such as the Cheviot Hills, the Lammermuirs were shaped by the master modeller of mountain form, the Ice Age. Completely covered by a moving and eventually melting ice sheet, the higher peaks were scoured flat, then deeply scarred by glacial meltwater, through which the Waters of Whiteadder, Blackadder, Leader, Dye, Monynut and Eye now flow.

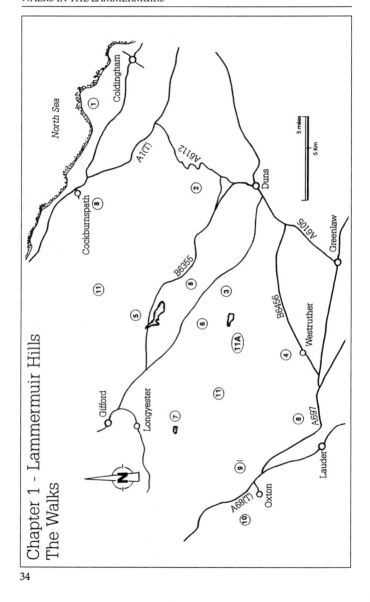

Chapter 1 - Lammermuir Hills
The Walks

Despite their lack of height the Lammermuirs provide a daunting hurdle to the traveller and have been so for two thousand years or more, whether on foot or assisted by the wheel. In the distant past when prehistoric man rambled by, and tree, scrub and bog covered the lower reaches and heather blackened the flat summits, the area was inhabited by wolves, wild boar and bear. Today these extinct creatures, plus the ever present sheep and black cattle, are remembered in the names of features on the map, such as Crow Stones, Hogs Law, Harecleugh, Wolfstruther, Hart Law and Hunt Law, Herd's Hill, Wedder Lairs, Collie Law and Cowhill.

The hills to the north are contained by a raised rim above the fertile lands of the Lothian plains, with Edinburgh a mere 20 miles/ 32km away; whereas the southern foothills fold gently into the 100,000 rich acres of the Tweeddale Merse, and the eastern bastion of towering seacliffs and stacs holds back the 'German Sea'. 27 miles/43.2km to the west, beyond Lauderdale, the boundary is marked by Gala Water and the A7(T). Entry to the range can be gained by three main roads and one minor road. Two thread along the extremities, the A1(T) Berwick to Edinburgh and the A7(T) Galashiels to Edinburgh. Of the roads that venture into the interior only two emerge successfully: the A68(T) Lauder to Dalkeith road, favoured by kings, clerics, armies, drovers, tinkers and travellers, and the B6355 Duns to Gifford road with its fierce gradients. An east-west traverse is only possible on foot.

Accommodation and refreshments for the walker are available a inns, bed and breakfasts, campsites and two youth hostels scattered around the upland fringes: clockwise from 1200hrs - Pathhead, Haddington, Gifford, Cockburnspath, Grantshouse, Coldingham, Chirnside, Duns, Greenlaw, Westruther and Lauder. Abbey St Bathans, Longformacus, Cranshaws and Oxton nestle in the interior.

The Lammermuirs are not 'huff and puff' hills and are best enjoyed on the many flat ridge walks in the steps of traders and the military along such ways as the Herring Road, with the tree-lined steep-sided valleys providing delightful alternatives. In fact many summits, without cairns or trig points, are traversed before the walker realises the top has been and gone. High fell and valley floor rich in social history offer a cornucopia of flora and fauna, plus an abundance of pleasing and varied views.

The absence of distinctive peaks and landmarks often leads to problems for the unwary walker, even in good visibility. With twenty or more look-alike summits between 1460ft/445m (Wedder Law) and 1755ft/535m (Meikle Says More), there is a need for navigational skills and country sense. Precipitation, a mean of 31 inches per year, whether in the form of hill fog or rain, is much lower than on the higher western Southern Uplands, thus making the Lammermuirs an ideal area for honing one's winter hill-walking and map-reading skills.

Public transport runs from:

Edinburgh to	-	Haddington, Berwick, Oxton, Pencaitland, Stow, Galashiels
Haddington to	-	Gifford, Humbie, Longyester, Garvald, Stenton, Dunbar
Galashiels to	-	Duns, Berwick, Westruther, Eyemouth
Post Bus	-	Duns to Longformacus

Timetables available at bus stations and tourist information centres.

THE WALKS

OS Maps: -   Landranger Series 1:50,000, Sheets 67, 73, 74.
Pathfinder 1:25,000, 421, 422, 423, 435, 436, 449.
One-inch Sheets 63, 62.

Walk 1 plunges headlong into the past with a short visit to mysterious Fast Castle on Wolf's Crag, high above the sea. Walk 2 proceeds more sedately with the curves of Whiteadder Water, to the intriguing Pictish phenomena of Edin's Hall Broch. Walk 3 rises from Longformacus, the Lammermuir capital, to the banks of Watch Water reservoir, the open grandstand of Scar Law and the tree-lined, bird-filled banks of Dye Water. Walk 4 tackles the battle hill of Twinlaw with its twin cairns and far distant views. Walk 5 pleases the eye and stimulates the body by ascending the prominent mass of Spartleton, above the shimmering waters of Whiteadder reservoir.

Walk 6 tramps a heathery path with only the feathered ones for

Edin's Hall Broch

company, from Killpallet to the Mutiny Stones, Dye Water and the Herring Road. Walk 7, the Hopes Adventure, circles the enclosed waters of Hopes reservoir, surrounded by lonely cleughs and the cairned summit of Lammer Law. Walk 8 traverses the Lammermuirs on the long distance path, the Southern Upland Way, from Lauder to Cockburnspath. Walk 9, from Carfraemill, walks the old trade route, via Crib Law and Lammer Law, from Lauderdale to the fertile acres of East Lothian. Walk 10 has the assistance of a Roman road, Dere Street, to a 12th century 'hospitum'. Walk 11 traverses the Lammermuirs to Lauder on the old way known as the Herring Road, a linear journey of 25 miles/40km, with a total ascent of 2264ft/690m. Walk 11A travels a slightly shorter version of an alternative Herring Road to Westruther. Both are walks of character and many surprises.

INFORMATION TABLE

WALK	DISTANCE Miles/Kilometres		ASCENT Feet/Metres		D of D *	TIME Hours
1	4	6.4	508	155	4	1¹/₂/2
2	3¹/₂	5.6	550	168	2	2
3	8³/₄	14	656	200	2	4¹/₂
4	10³/₄	17	843	257	2¹/₂	4¹/₂
5	5	8	760	232	2	2¹/₂/3
6	6¹/₂	10.4	750	229	3	3
7	4	6.4	300	91	1	2/2¹/₂
8	15¹/₄	24.5	1017	310	3	6¹/₂/7
8A	7	11.2	640	195	2	3/3¹/₂
8B	10¹/₄	16.5	459	140	2	4¹/₂/5
9	13³/₄	22	1175	358	3	7
10	4	6.4	328	100	2	2¹/₂
11	25	40	2264	690	4	10/11
11A	18¹/₂	29.6	2291	698	4	8/8¹/₂

*Degree of Difficulty

1 - Good path, no appreciable ascent, no navigational problems.
2 - Distinct path, noticeable ascents, longer walk.
3 - Paths rough or indistinct, ascent demanding, navigation required.
4 - Walk long, demanding compass and mountain skills, high exposure.

WALK 1: Wolf's Crag

GR 841696 - DOWLAW - TELEGRAPH HILL - FAST CASTLE - RETURN via DOWLAW - GR 841696

> *Say! dost thou hail from yonder cliffs so hoary -*
> *From yon rude caverned halls,*
> *Where strong Fast Castle, famed in olden story,*
> *Still lifts its ruined walls?*
>
> Walter Chisholm

*Fast Castle Head, a bastion of the eastern Lammermuirs, plunges headlong into the Firth of Forth with breathtaking intensity and provides a scenic experience of top quality. 4 miles/6.4km to and from the remains of the 'caste doune' towers of Fast Castle, a walk where time matters little, nor does the ascent of 508ft/155m. The grading of 4 is however of prime importance due to the high exposure on the approaches and on the unprotected summit of the stac. The route is signposted and takes the walker along grass verges and grassy paths, stepped in places, exposed in others, which in wet conditions can be slithery. Wear secure gripping footwear, **and if you are a vertigo sufferer or unsure on your feet, then view the castle from afar.***

To fully appreciate the primitive atmosphere of Fast Castle I suggest a walk during the nesting explosion of spring, or in the bronzed autumnal light accompanied by the seasonal roars of bull seals; and for the walker who has done it all, try it in a winter's storm with menacing banks of inky clag scudding in on a spiteful north-easter!

ROUTE DIRECTIONS

3 miles/4.8km east of the A1(T) and 6¹/₂ miles/10.4km west from Coldingham, on the A1107 Coldingham to Cockburnspath road, a minor road branches north-east, signposted 'Dowlaw 2 miles/ 3.2km'. Parking is possible, past the tower by Harly Darlies, just beyond the first cattle grid on a grassy clearing at GR 841696, taking care not to obstruct the farm track.

Walk east by bracken and gorse, parallel to the road and crossing the Soldier's Dyke, with the mound of Lowrie's Knowe and a weed-infested lochan on the right. Ahead is Dowlaw Farm, surrounded by the traditional shelter of trees, and beyond, Telegraph Hill (1) rears above the row of six farm cottages. At the second cattle grid turn left, between farm and conifers, descending past the cottages to the sign - 'Fast Castle'. Pass through the stone wall via a gate for a cliff-top walk that provides extensive and inspiring views of the East Lothian coastline, the Firth of Forth and the Kingdom of Fife capped by the Lomond Hills. Our grassy path winds by the angled wall on heather-clad cliffs below Telegraph Hill, to suddenly reveal the dramatic stac of Fast rising phoenix-like, alongside Wheat Stack Rock, from the surging waters far below. The path descends gradually, at first stepped, then becomes steeper as it curves left with the landward fence to narrow, within a few feet from the rim of the cliffs, where an unfenced couloir drops directly onto a bed of rocks far below. **WALK WARILY**. Once past, the way improves and continues seawards to the narrow concrete causeway, with its handrails of chain, connecting the stac summit of Fast Castle (2) to the cliffs.

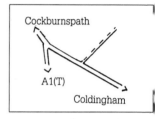

Underfoot amidst the castle ruins is a split-level sloping floor of grass and rock, protected only by a few blocks of crumbling masonry teetering on the exposed rim; scant protection between sea and watery oblivion. **GREAT CARE IS NEEDED.**

The return, via the outward route, enables the walker to admire the coastline and the moonscape of Coldingham Common.

Accommodation/refreshments at Coldingham, Grantshouse and Cockburnspath.

ITEMS OF INTEREST ALONG THE WAY

(1) TELEGRAPH HILL. An ideal site for relaying messages, either by fiery beacon or by radio transmission, to those in peril on land or sea. The steep cliffs high above the boiling sea by Fast Head were in the mid 1800s home to nesting ravens and peregrines.

(2) FAST CASTLE. Described under the pseudonym of Wolf's Crag in Walter Scott's *Bride of Lammermoor*. No records date the birth of a 'Donjon' on this exposed eyrie, though in the 1300s a stronghold on this site was recorded as being involved in Border conflict; and soon after Bannockburn it was brought to its knees by the English.

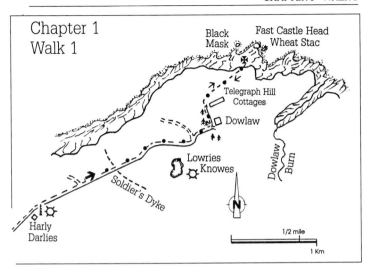

Chapter 1
Walk 1

Black Mask
Fast Castle Head
Wheat Stac
Telegraph Hill Cottages
Dowlaw
Lowries Knowes
Dowlaw Burn
Soldier's Dyke
N
Harly Darlies
1/2 mile
1 Km

Later, with the piratical William Holden in residence, it submitted yet again, this time in 1410 to the blades and blood of young Dunbar, and remained in Scottish hands for nigh on a century.

The 16th century brought great activity, but little good, to Fast Castle. A Scottish Warden, Sir Robert Ker, was murdered in 1513 by three Englishmen - Lilburn, Starkhead and Heron (known as The Bastard). Starkhead and Heron made good their escape, but Lilburn was captured, and in the absence of Heron the Bastard, James IV of Scotland took his brother, Heron of Ford Castle, and threw them both into the salty dungeons of Fast Castle, where they slowly starved to death. In the meantime Starkhead was murdered by a contract assassin of the Ker family, whilst James IV of Scotland lodged in Heron of Ford's castle prior to the battle of Flodden Field in September 1513, during which time, it is alleged, he seduced Heron of Ford's wife.

As if this was not enough, Fast Castle endured a further period of razing and rebuilding by both Scots and English. A comment as to its comfort was made in 1567 by the then English ambassador - "fitter to lodge prisoners in than folk at liberty as it is very small, so is it very strong". Finally, in the early 1600s, the castle faded into

41

oblivion along with the fortunes of its ultimate owners, the Logans of Restalrig. Its ultimate demise was hastened by the violent thunderstorm of 1871, which struck down a corbelled mass of masonry from the battlements of the crumbling keep.

WALK 2: The Pict's Way

GR 789609 - ELBA - EDIN'S HALL BROCH - ELLER BURN - ABBEY ST BATHANS

A choice of two delightfully stimulating walks, each of 3¹/₂ miles/5.6km ascending in the region of 550ft/168m above the beech-clad banks of winding Whiteadder Water on the south-eastern fringes of the Lammermuirs. One walk has a walk-in and a walk-out on the same path, the other is a linear walk. En route, Edin's Hall Broch (a rare pictish phenomenon in the Borders), Iron Age forts, the picturesque village of Abbey St Bathans and a multitude of wildlife grace these grade 2 walks of 2 hours' walking time. Best in the awakening of spring - the glad time, or the colourful russets of autumn. Walking boots/shoes are recommended.

ROUTE DIRECTIONS
The start is reached via the A6112, 3¹/₂ miles/5.6km south of Cockburnspath and 6 miles/9.6km north from Duns. Here a junction road signposted 'Abbey St Bathans' - 'Edins Hall Broch' turns west 200yds/m to the start at an angled bend in the road, GR 789609. Parking for 3 cars and a signpost 'Edin's Hall Broch - 1¹/₂ miles/ 2.4km, with yellow arrowheads on grey poles'.

A cart track leads south-west and at the first fork swing left, through a colourful mix of trees, parallel to Otter Burn. Several wooden cottages/holiday chalets are passed prior to crossing an undulating footbridge over the surging waters of Whiteadder, a favourite haunt of the colourful kingfisher, in the direction of Elba cottage (1). Just before the cottage is reached a waymarked path leads right through scrub into a gated riverside pasture. Follow the riverside fence west to a signposted dry-stone dyke, ascending left with the wall, crossing it via the waymarked stile. Continue rising west alongside a plantation where a lone pine marks the sign 'Broch on Crest of Hill, ¹/₂ mile/0.8km ahead'. Ascend through gorse, high

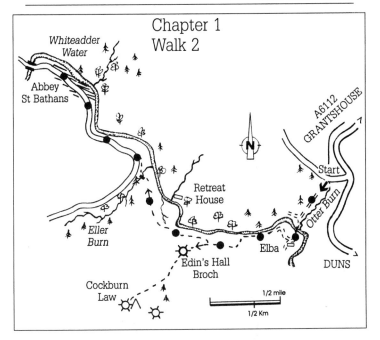

above the Whiteadder, to the huge stones of Edin's Hall Broch (2).

For a diversion to nearby Cockburn Law (3), traverse south-west over a pasture to a pine plantation, where several tracks west ascend the open fell to the summit from which fine views of Tweeddale, the Cheviots and the Lammermuirs can be enjoyed. Return to the Broch and for **Walk 1**, return to the start via the outward path, passing Elba.

For the linear alternative to Abbey St Bathans, leave the Broch via the track descending north-east to the pine plantation. Turn left and follow the path west and then north for ³/₄ mile / 1.2km descending to the confluence of Eller Burn and Whiteadder Water. Cross Eller Burn on a wooden footbridge then scramble up the woodside to a wicket gate, labelled 'Public Footpath', onto the Abbey St Bathans road, where a large metal sign says 'TOOT'. Descend right, with the road, for ³/₄ mile / 1.2km to the pleasing waterside village of Abbey

St Bathans (4). For refreshment and relaxation there is the Riverside Cafe by Whiteadder Water footbridge and ford.

Accommodation/refreshment at Duns and Abbey St Bathans.

ITEMS OF INTEREST ALONG THE WAY

(1) ELBA COTTAGE. There are three theories as to why it was called Elba.

   a) It was built in Napoleonic times, in the years of the Emperor's exile on the island of Elba.
   b) Derived from the Gaelic, *Eil* - hill and *Both* - dwelling.
   c) It is built on a sharp bend in the river, the local name for such a bend being elbow, pronounced locally as 'Elba'.

I like c) best. Nearby are the remains of a copper mine of the 1700s.

(2) EDIN'S HALL BROCH. A unique pictish structure, high above Whiteadder Water on the flanks of Cockburn Law. Surrounded by ovoid earthworks, built of immense blocks of whinstone, its basic remains are circular measuring 90ft/27m in exterior diameter, with walls varying in thickness from 15 to 19ft/4.5 to 5.8m, and rising to 6ft/2m. Within this massive wall five chambers lead from either the single gateway or the central courtyard. Only five Brochs exist outside the Highlands and Islands; Edin's Hall, the largest, has suffered, as have many others, from "the rude hand of ignorance or agriculture".

(3) COCKBURN LAW 1066ft/325m. If legend and folklore is your forte, then away to the ditches and earthworks of Cockburn Law, where three theories are still discussed as to the origins of the visible remains that pockmark the hill. Was it a stronghold of the legendary giant Red Etin/Edin, a temple to the god Woden, or perhaps a Druid sanctuary?

(4) ABBEY ST BATHANS. Named after Bothan, a 7th century Prior of Old Mailros, this pleasing hamlet stands by the tree-lined banks of the Whiteadder. Within its bounds there remains a ruined priory, the site of a chapel, and a spring whose waters were reputed to heal all sickness, in addition to "neither fogging nor freezing".

WALK 3: The Water Round

LONGFORMACUS - WATCH WATER RESERVOIR - SCAR LAW - DYE COTTAGE - DYE WATER - LONGFORMACUS

A circular walk of great charm, on the southern flanks of the Lammermuir plateau. Waymarked for much of its 8³/₄ miles/14km it has a barely noticed height gain of 656ft/200m as it trips along burnside lanes, grassy fell paths and heathery tracks, including a picturesque section of the Southern Upland Way by Watch Water. Graded 2, this 4¹/₂ hour hike travels through three differing eco-cultures, providing for the observant a wide selection of wildlife, in particular birdlife. Keep an eye open for the soaring buzzard. For comfort, walking shoes/boots are recommended.

ROUTE DIRECTIONS

Longformacus, GR 693572, a hamlet of some charm but little sustenance, nestles by Dye Water 8 miles / 12.8km west-north-west from Duns, connected by a minor road leading off the A6105. Free parking in the village is available, but take care not to block access. Start the walk south of the Dye Water bridge where a signpost indicates west on the waymarked SUW (Southern Upland Way) to Watch Water reservoir (1), a picturesque tree section, albeit somewhat hard on the feet, before reaching the grass verges of the Lammermuir foothills. Once at the lamb-chop reservoir of Watch Water the SUW skirts the north shore passing the deserted beech-sheltered farm of Scarlaw. Continue south-west for 600yds/m on the grassy path, noting the distinctive cairns of Twin Law marking the skyline ahead. At the first junction turn sharp right to leave the SUW.

Our route now ascends and descends north, on a grass and in places stony track for 1¹/₂ miles / 2.4km, over the heathery head of Scar Law into the stillness of Dye Water valley. A pause on the ridge of Scar Law provides extensive views south of the fertile Merse, the wide Tweed valley and the gangling Cheviot Hills.

The robust Dye Water is crossed via a stone bridge to Dye Cottage, where our way turns sharp right onto a stony path running east between the musical waters and the cottage of Dye. An interesting and scenically pleasing pathway (as per the OS map) follows Dye Water (2) for 2 miles / 3.2km east and south-east into Longformacus (3). The valley is steep sided and in places narrow.

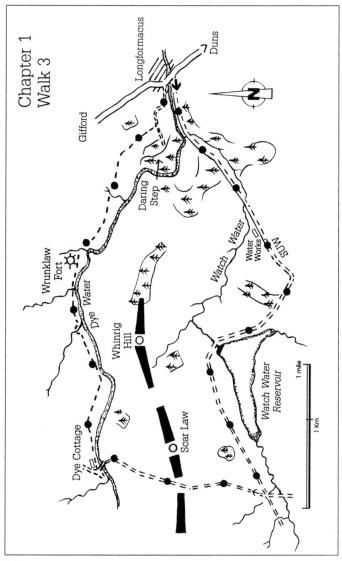

Chapter 1
Walk 3

Longformacus

Duns

Gifford

Daring Step

Wrunklaw Fort

Watch Water

Water Works

SUW

Dye Water

Whinrig Hill

Dye Cottage

Scar Law

Watch Water Reservoir

1 mile

1 Km

To the south the steep flanks of Whinrig Hill tumble sharply down to the waterside and on warm days provide spirals of warm air so beloved by the wheeling birds of prey. Several small feeder burns surge in from the left before the Iron Age fort on Wrunklaw's southern rim is passed (marked on OS map); the sharp ascent to the earthworks is worthwhile.

Sadly the path changes character as it threads its damp way through rush and moss before swinging left and ascending north-east with Horseupcleugh Burn, before forking right through a field gate to contour the hillside first south and then south-east. An animal food store acts as a useful waymark, as the path continues to rise above Dye Water to two small knowes on the skyline ahead. The path, a few degrees south of east, leaves the riverside rising steadily above the tree-clad cliffs to the right. Pass by two knowes, walking east by Sinclair's Hill, above the steep wooded bank of Daring Step before swinging south-east between two fingers of trees for 500yds/462m to Manse Road. Turn and descend left, ie. east, as it zigzags into Longformacus.

Limited accommodation in Longformacus, a wider range in Duns.

ITEMS OF INTEREST ALONG THE WAY

(1) WATCH WATER RESERVOIR. Created in 1954, by flooding a small area of the Watch Water valley. Small and picturesque it stands with the reservoirs of Whiteadder and Hope as the only expanses of water of any substance in the Lammermuirs. Vaulting from the ruins of Scarlaw Tower, now underwater, supports the west gable of Scarlaw Cottage.

(2) DYE WATER WILDLIFE. On the surrounding moorland curlew, golden plover and lapwing summer, whilst snipe frequent the bogs at home in the rushes. At water level herons silently stand and oyster catchers shriek, whilst ring ouzel, wheatear and whinchat flit, chirping from stone to stone. And as the timid titling peeps in the heather the cuckoo's cry heralds summer.

(3) LONGFORMACUS. 'A place of pools', long regarded as the 'capital of the Lammermuirs' and alleged to be either Celtic or Anglican in origin. Folk tales tell us that Sinclair of Roslin was the laird of 'Longfordmakehous' in the late 14th century and his tower was built ½ mile/0.8km upwater above the Dye. The tower was

abandoned after the tragic death of the young son and another built; the last Sinclairs sold the estates in 1764. For a full account of life in 19th century Longformacus I recommend the booklet *Glimpses into the Past in the Lammermuirs* by John Hutton Browne.

WALK 4: The Battle Hill

WESTRUTHER - WEDDERLIE - CRALAW - TWIN LAW - SOUTHERN UPLAND WAY TO TWINLAW WOOD - CRALAW - WESTRUTHER

The conspicuous, coned and cairned summit of Twin Law dominates the southern rim of the Lammermuir Hills, a few miles north of Westruther. Although no higher than 1467ft/447m, and not by any stretch of the imagination a 'huff and puff' hill, it is for a Lammermuir, obtrusive. To reach Twinlaw Cairns involves a linear, return with loop, trip of 10³/₄ miles/17km and gradual total height gain of 843ft/257m. Underfoot roadside verges, concrete strips, grassy cart tracks and paths through heather require lightweight walking boots/shoes for this 4¹/₂ hour journey graded 2¹/₂ or an easy 3. A rewarding historic walk for a clear day, with moorland birds and plants providing good company, and the views, in particular on the return trip, at times spectacular across the Tweed valley to the Cheviots.

ROUTE DIRECTIONS

Start at the hamlet of Westruther (1), GR 602476, on the B6456 11¹/₂ miles / 18.4km west of Duns. Parking is available alongside the church (not on Sundays please) and at a small car park at the east end of the village.

Walk east with the B6456, a quiet road with a grassy verge, to Wedderlie lane end, turning left, ie. north, along a sylvan avenue to Wedderlie Farm. Two forks are met; bear left at each one before the tarmac changes into twin concrete strips leading to the lone and lonely cottage of Cralaw. Continue north with the track over open fells, the silence broken by singing lark and plaintive whaup, to a gated wire fence.

Just beyond the gate leave the main track north by taking the pathway rising left, ie. west, a curving way that started life as a

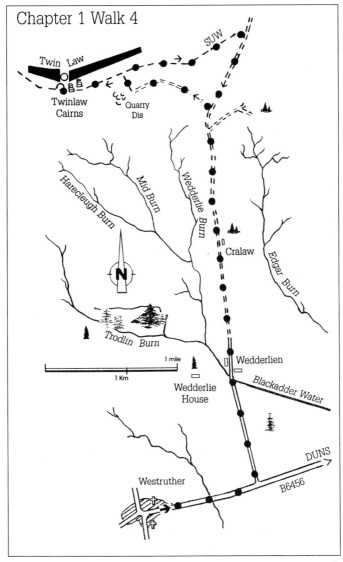

Chapter 1 Walk 4

Twin Law

Twinlaw Cairns

SUW

Quarry Dis

Harecleugh Burn

Mid Burn

Wedderlie Burn

N

Cralaw

Edgar Burn

Trodlin Burn

1 mile

1 Km

Wedderlie House

Wedderlien

Blackadder Water

Westruther

DUNS

B6456

Twinlaw Cairns - east one

quarry road. Up to this point the walker may have had glimpses of the twin cairns on Twin Law summit. From here to the final few yards the cairns are hidden from view on the centre of the flat top. The old quarry road leads to a gated stone dyke. Pass through and turn right by the disused quarries ascending north via the wall to a SUW (Southern Upland Way) stile. Do not cross but veer left, ie. west, with the heathery SUW to the summit supporting the large and unusual Twinlaw Cairns (2); they provide a unique resting and viewing facility, plus visitors book, sheltered from the north wind and opening out over the extensive and fruitful acres of Tweeddale.

Return east from Twin Law summit, no doubt after a refreshment stop, to the stile. Cross and follow the waymarked SUW path east and north-east through heather and white grass for 1 mile / 1.6km to the square coniferous plantation known as Twinlaw Wood. At the junction with a southbound track pass right through the gate ascending gradually south and south-south-east for $^3/_4$ mile / 1.2km to the quarry track by the gated fence of our outward journey.

Return south via Cralaw and Wedderlie, on the descending pathway with the extending views, for the return to Westruther.

Accommodation/refreshments available in Duns and Westruther.

ITEMS OF INTEREST ALONG THE WAY

(1) WESTRUTHER. "The swamp of the wolves - Wolfstruther", this hamlet arose in an area of great woods inhabited by wild beasts; today there are few woods and no wild beasts. The ivy-clad ruins of a Covenanting Kirk stand in the centre of the old kirk yard, a church that was in the 17th century sanctuary for "Vietch of Westruther", a hell-fire preacher of Berwickshire.

(2) TWIN LAW & TWINLAW CAIRNS. $5^{3}/_{4}$ miles/9.2km south-east of Twin Law summit The Kaims can be seen, an exceptional line of glacial debris writhing east/west for more than 2 miles/3.2km. Resembling military firing ranges, they are, however, one of the finest examples of an Esker - Scandinavian for winding banks of sand and gravel, marking sub-glacial streams - in Scotland.

The two identical cairns on Twin Law were originally erected to commemorate two members of the local and ancient Edgar family, young men who were slain in a battle whilst fighting, unknowingly, on opposite sides. Two verses from the anonymous ballad *The Battle of Twin Law* describe well the catastrophy.

> *Oh, curst be the sword, my dear brother.*
> *That wounded thee sae deep;*
> *A weary tryst we've had this day*
> *And side by side we'll sleep.*
> *And they spake nae word when a' was dune,*
> *That had be sae fierce afore;*
> *But the tane gaed back o'er the Cheviot hill*
> *And the tithers keept the Lammermuir.*

Polish tanks, training in the Lammermuirs during World War Two, demolished the original Twin Cairns in 1944. The present imposing cairns were raised from the rubble by a Berwickshire 'dyker' after the war ended.

WALK 5: Spartleton Direct

WHITEADDER RESERVOIR GR 646642 - GAMELSHIEL CASTLE - SPARTLETON RIDGE - SPARTLETON - GAMELSHIEL CASTLE - GR 646642

The 760ft/232m ascent of heather-clad Spartleton, an outstanding landmark and rewarding grandstand, covers 5 circular miles/8km over stony cart tracks and sections of grassy twin track between the ever present heather. Passing en route the sad ruined stones of Gamelshiel Castle, the way is enlivened by glimpses of the many differing faces of south-east Scotland, with the glistening waters of Whiteadder reservoir continuously in view for the descent. Wear clothing appropriate for the weather conditions, both overhead and underfoot, for this grade 2 walk of 2^1/2/3 hours.

ROUTE DIRECTIONS

Whiteadder, the largest of the Lammermuir reservoirs (1), provides the start / finish at its north-west corner, where parking is available on the grass verges of the B6355 above the head of the reservoir at GR 643643, or in the layby alongside the conifers and starting gate east of the bridge, GR 646642.

As the gate is padlocked (for vehicles only) cross the cushioned wire fence adjacent to the gate and walk north-north-west on a stony track (not marked on OS map) between the reservoir and the trees to the sheep pens below Summer Hill. At the pens swing left ascending east with a stony track by a feeder burn, soon to reach the two remaining sadly scarred walls of Gamelshiel Castle (2).

After inspection continue to ascend east betwixt burn and fence on a grassy path that leaves the pasture fence and accompanying burn as the heather line is met, beyond which yet another guiding fence on the right assists the steep pathway to a gated crossroads on Spartleton's south-east ridge. Turn left, ie. north-west, to ascend a sandy, peaty and in places grassy twin track through the surrounding heather; an ascent to the summit that appears more severe to the eye than it actually is on the legs. Just below the summit scan the heather to the right, for a track branching north, for the final easy yards to the trig point on the flat summit of Spartleton. Though this typical Lammermuir hill lacks a foot or two in height it certainly lacks nothing in visual delights (3), offering the walker the most pleasing

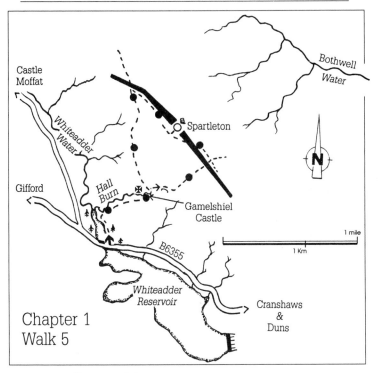

Castle
Moffat

Bothwell
Water

Whiteadder
Water

Spartleton

N

Gifford

Hall
Burn

Gamelshiel
Castle

B6355

1 mile

1 Km

Whiteadder
Reservoir

Cranshaws
&
Duns

Chapter 1
Walk 5

views on all points of the compass.

For the descent, walk with the track north and then north-west for ¹/₂ mile/0.8km, hopefully enjoying the sights directly ahead of the Firth of Forth and the Kingdom of Fife, to join a bridleway (shown on the OS map) running north to south on the western flanks of Spartleton. At the junction turn sharp left, ie. south, to descend with this grassy way for 1 mile/1.6km to Gamelshiel Castle. A delightful section, with stimulating views of the patchwork of hills that closet Whiteadder Water as it enters and leaves the shimmering surface of Whiteadder reservoir far below.

From Gamelshiel Castle and its prickly carpet of nettles and thistles descend west with the outward stony road to the starting gate by the reservoir and the B6355.

Accommodation and refreshments at Gifford and Cranshaws.

ITEMS OF INTEREST ALONG THE WAY

(1) WHITEADDER RESERVOIR. The largest of the Lammermuir reservoirs, it was operational from 1969, and is run by the East of Scotland Water supplying the Edinburgh area.

(2) GAMELSHIEL CASTLE. One of six towers or strongholds that at one time stood proudly by the banks of Whiteadder Water, stretching from its source to the confluence with Dye Water. Today only Cranshaws remains and in the case of Gamelshiel all that remains are the crumbling remnants of two walls, a condition exacerbated perhaps as much by the hand of agriculture as by Hertford, the border butcher.

Of the former occupants little is known, but a tale is told of a previous lady of Gamelshiel who walked the slopes of Spartleton one summer's evening where "a great wolf set upon her and worried her".

(3) VIEWS from SPARLETON. To the north the Firth of Forth, Bass Rock *et al* and beyond, Kingdom and the 'Paps' of Fife; and should the air be clear the southern peaks of the Highland line. To the south the entire Cheviot ridge fills the skyline past the twin domes of Dirrington and the Tweed valley; whilst the western quadrant presents the Lammermuir plateau and the distant hazy ranges of Tweedsmuir and the Pentlands.

WALK 6: The Devil's Work

GR 635612 - CHARTERIS' WELL - KILLPALLET - MUTINY STONES - BYERCLEUGH - TROTTINGSHAW - LAMB HILL - GR 636612

A circular 6¹/₂ miles/10.4km walk with a height gain of 750ft/229m, over heathery fells and by the narrow bends of Dye Water in the emptiness of the central Lammermuirs, passing en route old whisky stills, a Stone Age burial site and the Herring Road. This 3 hour experience, graded 3 (map and compass skills are essential in certain parts should visibility suddenly deteriorate) can be enjoyed by all if the day is sunny. Walking shoes/boots are recommended as is warm waterproof clothing in inclement conditions.

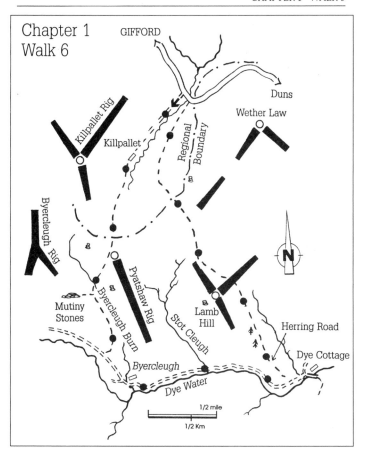

This is a grand walk over wild country, but a word of advice before you start. Even though the way is marked on the OS map as a footpath it traverses the property of others who live and work on these moors. Grouse rearing and shooting is practised so I would ask you to respect others' property, sticking to the paths during the spring nesting season and avoiding this walk from August 12th to December 10th.

ROUTE DIRECTIONS

Start at GR 635612, a lonely spot on the Berwickshire/East Lothian boundary, hemmed in by heavy moorland, 5 miles/8km north-west of Longformacus on an unclassified road just beyond the huge stones of 'The Grey Mare' and 'The Grey Mare's Foal', and 3½ miles/5.6km south-east from the junction of the B6355 Gifford to Duns road. At an elbowed bend in the road, over Killpallet Burn and below a cattle grid, there is a parking space for three or four cars.

Commence by crossing the burn and leaving the road left, walking south-south-west on a twin tracked farm road, leading up the tight valley of Killpallet. ¾ mile/1.2km ahead are the cottages and steading of Killpallet (1), surrounded by a sea of green green grass. Along the track the remains of Charteris' Well, and east of the burn the grooves and gullies of the Herring Road, our return route, can be seen. The compact steading of old Killpallet is soon left behind as the path forks left and ascends south to the skyline, passing a deep cleugh on the left. The higher the rutted track goes the narrower it becomes, in places almost disappearing under encroaching heather. Continue ascending, a degree or two west of south, to a slip rail in the post and wire fence on the skyline - Scottish Borders Boundary. Scan the moorland west and south, beyond the deep and narrow valley of Dye, where it appears every single top has at least one cairn adorning the skyline: Titling Cairn, Rutherford's Cairn, Twinlaw Cairns, and Dunside Hill Cairn, to mention but a few.

Leave the fence on a thin trace through the acres of continuous heather over Pyatshaw Ridge, bearing 208° magnetic, with a prominent cairn 600yds/554m ahead due south as a marker. The variable narrow path snakes round humps and hollows in the 700yd/646m descent to Byercleugh Burn, but at all times maintain the bearing and/or keep the marker cairn to your left. Once the cairn is reached look west over Byercleugh Burn to the south-eastern side of Byercleugh Ridge, where a gargantuan pile of stones (reputed to have been dropped by the Devil), known now as the Mutiny Stones (2), can be seen. Cross the moss and rush infested cleugh on a narrow sheep track, on a line west from the marker cairn to the Mutiny Stones/Long Cairn, GR 624590, that lie above and 200yds/185m west from the burn.

Mutiny Stones - Long Cairn

Return east to the burnside. Do not cross but turn right, ie. south, where a path on the true right bank leads to a waterfall by two trees. At this point the ¹/₂ mile/0.8km path to the stilted tin shed leaves the burn and its ever deepening gully. The ancient path south now lies beneath a variable covering of heather; for experienced 'heather loupers' it is not difficult to profile the path's outline, for other mortals the bearing is 194° magnetic or the strip of conifers of Dunside Hill south across Dye Water. As the tin shed is approached the solid heather gives way to white grass revealing a westwards pathway to the valley road. Swing left with this road and descend to Byercleugh.

A narrow tarmac road, snaking east along the valley floor, leaves the wooden dwellings of Byercleugh, in company with the hurrying and at times noisy Dye Water. Grass verges cushion the footfalls to make the 1¹/₂ miles/2.4km to Trottingshaw a delightful valley walking experience, for Dye valley is a lonely and beautiful place wedged between encroaching shoulders of moorland; a place for herons, dippers and migratory ring ousels (known in this area as ring starlings).

Just prior to the road-fork at Dye Cottage, Trottingshaw Burn and a wide farm track unexpectedly tumble in from the left. Take this track left, ie. north-west, as it ascends with the visible raised and gouged way of the old Herring Road (3). Continue ascending north-north-west over Lamb Hill then down to Killpallet: $2^3/4$ miles/ 4.4km of invigorating walking, with moorland birds (4) for company, encouraging a brisk pace and a light step. Navigation is easy, with the visible remains of the Herring Road close by or underfoot, for the entire length. On the descent to Killpallet tramp the old roadway, and when it joins with the fence a few hundred yards from journey's end swing right and descend north on the Herring Road on the right side of the wire fence to reach the gate close by the starting point.

Limited accommodation at Longformacus, a wider selection at Duns or Gifford.

ITEMS OF INTEREST ALONG THE WAY

(1) KILLPALLET. In the 1800s spelt Kilpallet, a lonely farm originally with a triplet of trees, one ash two plane; only the ash remains. In the 18th and 19th centuries one of the many outby farms operating illicit whisky stills and hiding the resultant spirit on nearby Byercleugh Ridge. Whisky production proved to be a valuable addition to the upland purse, approved by the majority of the rural community, the exception of course being the Gaugers or Excisemen.

(2) MUTINY STONES. Legend has it they were the Devil's work, falling from his mittens as he passed overhead, and were originally named "Mittenfu of Stones" as seen on Stobie's map of 1794. This name was later corrupted to Meeting Stones and then distorted by clerical error to the present Mutiny Stones. Stone Age in origin this Long Cairn, more common in the north-west of Scotland and North Tynedale, is the only one of its type in Berwickshire. Scattered east to west across the 1250ft/381m contour line, the Long Cairn is constructed of local stones 278ft/85m long, 76ft/23m wide at the east end and 20ft/6m at the west end, with a height of $11^1/2$ft/3.5m at its east end and 3ft/0.9m at its west end. This burial cairn has been sadly mutilated by robbing holes and the removal of stones for

agricultural purposes.

(3) HERRING ROAD. A centuries-old road running south from the herring port of Dunbar, much used by fish-cadgers and borderfolk for the transportation of herring. The still visible V shaped gouges were made by teams of laden pack-horses constantly following the same path over the Lammermuirs. The 'Road' clambers over Lothian Edge into the heart of the Lammermuirs at Kingside Hill beside Whiteadder Water, where it splits into two routes. The main route winds south-west ascending to Little Says Law before the long descent to Lylestone Hill and Lauder - **Walk 11**; the other continues south with Faseny Water via Watch Water to Wedderlie and Westruther - **Walk 11A**.

(4) MOORLAND BIRDS. Summer provides fine company for the walker with the curlew, golden plover, lapwing (peewit) and snipe brightening the skyline and pleasing the ear. In winter the hills appear to be devoid of life, save for the staccato cry of 'Go Back Go Back' from disturbed grouse, and sightings of wandering flocks of snow buntings.

WALK 7: The Hopes Adventure

HOPES WATER STATION GR 558633 - WEST HOPES - HOPES RESERVOIR - HOPES WATER - WEST HOPES - GR 558633

Below the circlet of the Hope Hills lie the secluded and seductive waters of Hopes reservoir; hills and water so fine of form, they are without doubt the jewel in the Lammermuir crown. Walk 7 is for those who wish to drink deep from the scenic cup that is the Hopes Adventure. A gentle and picturesque grade 1 circuit of the reservoir and glen, covering 4 miles/6.4km in 2/2¹/₂ hours, with a minimal height gain of 300ft/91m on farm and waterside roads and heathery paths. Walking boots/shoes for comfort.

ROUTE DIRECTIONS
From the crossroads 2¹/₂ miles/4km east of Gifford via the B6355 a signpost 'Newlands, Quarryford and Longyester' points right, ie. south, then south-west. 2 miles/3.2km along this winding lane, on the left fork beyond Quarryford, and just east of Longyester, a sign

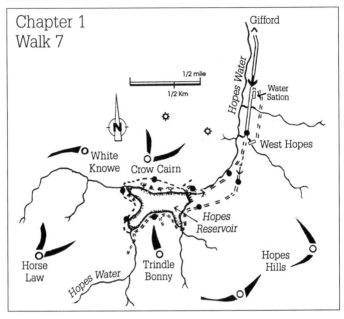

Chapter 1
Walk 7

by the school, 'Hopes 1¹/₄ mile', points left, ie. south-south-east, via a single track to the Water Authority station, GR 558633, beyond Hopes House. Parking available but please do not block access.

From the water station walk south, through the wicket gate by the cottage, for ¹/₂ mile/0.8km to the steading of West Hopes, with exciting prospects of steep-sided hills ahead. Just prior to the farm keep on the southbound track, crossing the stile by the gate, then veer left onto the higher of the two grass and dirt roads leading south-west above Hopes Water. The dam of Hopes reservoir can now be seen with the black and shapely backdrop of the Laws of Bleak and Lammer on the western skyline. Continue west with the grassy track as it winds along the water's edge, first into a small tree-lined inlet fed by a picturesque cleugh, then to a second and larger inlet leading south to the source of Hopes Water. The surrounding banks present a balanced and colourful mix of trees, shrubs, ground cover and wildlife (1).

At the southern apex of the second inlet the wide track continues south to follow Hopes Water between Windy Law and Trindle Bonny. At this point we leave the track and descend to cross Hopes Water and ascend steeply on a narrow heather-bound path that contours above the water close to an ageing reservoir fence. Go north and then west, past a small coniferous stand, to the head of the reservoir, fed by Sting Bank Burn. To the left the curving sweep of Sting Bank glen can be seen below the upper reaches of Lammer Law, the second highest Lammermuir. Descend right and cross the burn to a distinct but narrow path some 20ft/6m above.

Turn right and pass through a wicket gate into the trees (1), a Site of Special Scientific Interest, onto a pathway running east above the reservoir. This is a way of visual rewards, travelling as it does first through well-spaced trees then opening out over banks of heather for nearly ¹/₂ mile/0.8km, before tapering down to the north end of the dam. A stile leads over the fence to the dam, with its interesting spillway and bridge (2). Once at the dam a wide grass track winds down to below the embankment, passing various reservoir devices (please observe the Water Authority notices regarding public water supplies) to continue east with Hopes Water, through banks of broad-leaved trees. Cross two stiles and emerge at West Hopes. Above, to the right, are the bulky rims of the Hope Hills topped by Harestone Hill with its massive Whitestone Cairn. Continue north on the road to the end of the journey at GR 558633.

Accommodation and refreshments at the charming village of Gifford.

ITEMS OF INTEREST ALONG THE WAY

(1) FLORA & FAUNA. On the flanks of the hills, surrounding the reservoir, heather and bracken abound; the bell-heather shines bright in July and August, whilst the hills are ablaze with a purple carpet of ling from August. Autumn and spring bring forth the golds, reds and greens of the bracken. In the cleughs and by the rocky burns thyme bursts forth and the banks of the reservoir are clothed with alder, willow, dog rose, silver birch, rowan, beech, ash, juniper, Scots pine, and spruce. Ahead a heron flails into flight with the squawking terns, whilst higher on the hill a buzzard soars and swoops above hen harrier, curlew, peewit, ring ouzel and grouse. Highest of all, screaming swifts circle above Lammer Law. Rabbits

are in profusion, mountain hares abound and evidence can be seen of the wary fox.

(2) RESERVOIR SPILLWAY & BRIDGE. The fine stone bridge leading over the spillway and its retaining walls bears the inscription

"THEARCHOFTHISBRIDGEANDTHEWALLSOFTHEWATER-COURSEOVERWHICHITSTANDSWEREBROUGHT-FROMTHECALTONJAILEDINBURGHWHICHWASDEMOLISHED-IN1930-31".

WALK 8: The Southern Upland Way

LAUDER - BRAIDSHAWRIG - TWIN LAW - LONGFORMACUS - WHITCHESTER - ABBEY ST BATHANS - WHITEBURN - PEASE BURN - COCKBURNSPATH

The Southern Upland Way (SUW) is a challenging long distance path, of approximately 202 miles/323km, winding through the Southern Uplands from Portpatrick on the west coast to Cockburnspath overlooking the east coast. It enters the Lammermuir Hills at Lauder and traverses east-north-east in three sections, which can, by the energetic, be condensed into two sections. It provides the Lammermuir walker with a choice of two or three days' continuous walking, or three separate walks to be undertaken over countryside that varies from wild open moorland to wooded and pastoral sections before finally arriving at Berwickshire's coast.

The longest section is Lauder to Longformacus, covering 15¼ miles/ 24.5km over open fell and exposed moorland although with no too-severe ascents. The rewards are commensurate with the effort, for the views from Twin Law are considered by many as the finest of the entire journey. All sections are waymarked by the Thistle Emblem, with stiles and gates at fences/dykes, plus many items of interest along the way. Hill-walking footwear and clothing are essential, as are map and compass skills, especially in winter conditions or poor visibility.

ROUTE DIRECTIONS
Walk 8 - Section One, Lauder to Longformacus. 15¼ miles/24.5km.

From the centre of Lauder walk south-east with the A68(T), turning left at the gatehouse and stable block leading to the grounds of

Chapter 1
Walk 8

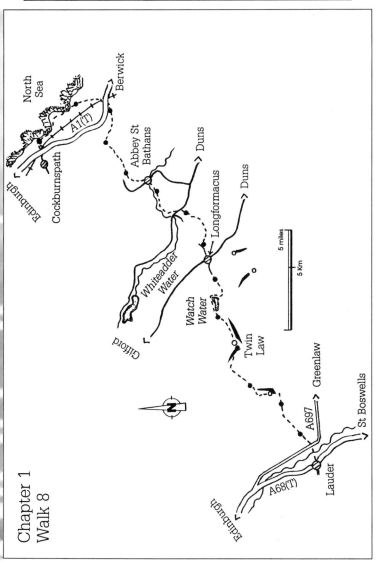

Thirlestane Castle (1). This is a pleasant section that crosses Leader Water, and with frequent waymarks, passes through woodland to cross the A697 and rise to Wanton Walls Farm. Beyond, the track rises with dykes and stiles to Snawdon Burn to eventually join a track above Blythe Water; there are more stiles as the way descends to a wooden bridge (2) over the burn.

Ascend the eastern bank and at the fork swing left on the way to Scoured Rig. From here descend through the trees to the lonely farm of Braidshawrig. Dramatic isolation now surrounds our route as Twin Law dominates the skyline ahead and heather is all around. By track and fenceside path the twin cairns on Twin Law summit (3) are reached.

Now travelling mainly east the recently raised footpath descends, via John Dippie's Well, to Watch Water reservoir; beyond which the pastoral scene and the tarmac are rejoined and the way saunters by shaded burnside into Longformacus (4).

All facilities at Lauder, limited accommodation only at Longformacus.

Walk 8A - Section Two, Longformacus to Abbey St Bathans. 7 miles/11.2km. An easy and short route with well-placed waymarks, over the lower reaches of the Lammermuirs, where trees and an increasing number of fences are met as are the eye-catching tree-lined banks of Whiteadder Water. Leave Longformacus with the signpost "Ellemford and Whitchester', and once over Blacksmill Burn leave the road for pastures green at the waymark. Follow the waymarks east, ascending the grassy moor and heading east via an L-shaped stand of conifers before skirting Owl Wood. At Commonside Wood, by the hill top, join a descending track through Lodge Wood to the B6355; turn left to Whitchester Lodge (5).

Continue on the road past the lodge for 100yds/m, then turn right at the waymark rising with track and path above Whiteadder Water, our companion via Robber's Cleugh and Roughside Wood to Abbey St Bathans (6).

Accommodation and refreshments at Abbey St Bathans.

Walk 8B - Section Three, Abbey St Bathans to Cockburnspath. 10¹/₄ miles/16.5km. A mix of cart tracks, paths, and public road, with a word of caution for the final coastal path in poor visibility and

Ernescleugh Water (Ch.1. Walk 11)
Whiteadder Water reservoir (Ch.1. Walk 11A)

Dunslair Heights (Ch.2. Walk 9)

Whitehope Law from Lee Pen (Ch.2. Walk 12)

strong winds. Cross Whiteadder north, ascending above the confluence of the Waters of Monynut and Whiteadder to follow a drove road to a bridge over Whare Burn. This burn acts as guide to Blakestone Moor leading in turn to Whiteburn Farm, then north to join a minor public road.

Turn left with this road for a few hundred yards before striking north-east cross-country, via Blackburn Mill and Blackburn, to reach Pease Burn (7) and the A1(T). Turn left and cross the busy A1(T), perhaps the most hazardous steps in the Lammermuirs, to enter Penmanshiel forest, a mish-mash of tracks as the way ascends high above Pease Dean (with its information shelter). Ahead, Pease Bay, Cove and Cove Harbour beckon as descent is made and the A1107 is crossed, rejoining Pease Burn as it heads seawards by Pease Bay Caravan Site to the North Sea which is almost, but not quite, journey's end. A bay of red, from the outcrops of Old Red Sandstone, is left for a final climb and a cliff-top walk (8) to Cove and journey's end at Cockburnspath's mercat cross (9).

Accommodation and refreshments at Cockburnspath.

ITEMS OF INTEREST ALONG THE WAY

(1) THIRLESTANE CASTLE. The present castle, on the site of Edward II's fort, was built at the end of the 1500s and later became the seat of the Dukes of Lauderdale.

(2) BLYTHE WATER BRIDGE. Built by the OTC of Edinburgh and Heriot-Watt universities in 1985, to replace a previous one that was cast 300yds/m downstream during the disastrous floods of November 1984.

(3) TWIN LAW. A grandstand that reveals the lower Tweed valley, the Cheviot range and the North Sea, in addition to being topped by the unique Twinlaw Cairns (**Walk 4**). The cairns were erected in memory of two brothers who perished whilst fighting, unknowingly, one for the attacking Saxons, the other for the defending Scots. Each cairn has a sheltered recessed seat, one also has a visitors book.

(4) LONGFORMACUS. The 'capital' of the Lammermuirs, whose original church dated back to 1243, is a pleasing picturesque village with unfortunately few creature comforts to offer the long distance wayfarer.

(5) WHITCHESTER LODGE. Bears an inscription "AS and IFL 1897", the initials of Andrew Smith and Ida F. Landale, his wife; the family motto was "By war and wit".

(6) ABBEY ST BATHANS. Seat of an ancient Cistercian nunnery, and dedicated to a cousin of Columba, who succeeded him at the monastery on Iona. Sadly the nunnery suffered total destruction when Hertford cut his bloody swath through the Borders in 1545 (**Walk 2**).

(7) PEASE BURN. An extract from a lament to the banks of Pease Burn 1547 reads "that who goeth straight doune salbe in daunger of tumbling, and the cummer up so, sure of puffing and payne:".

(8) COASTAL VIEWS. Some 16 miles/25.6km north-west, rising out of the Firth of Forth, the conical mass of Bass Rock, home to St Baldred in the 7th century, prison to prominent Covenanters in the 17th century, and today perhaps the best gannetry in Britain. To the south the headlands of Siccar Point, one of Scotland's geological 'bedrocks' around which James Hutton based his *Theory of the Earth*, 1795; plus Fast Castle Head on which the remains of Fast Castle teeter (**Walk 1**).

(9) COCKBURNSPATH. A village referred to in the early 12th century, it records that its "mercat cross was erected by James IV of Scotland in 1503 in celebration of his marriage to Princess Margaret Tudor, to whom he presented the Lands of Cockburnspath as a dowry".

WALK 9: The Gold Trail

CARFRAEMILL - KELPHOPE VALLEY - TOLLISHILL - CRIB LAW - LAMMER LAW - TOLLISHILL & KELPHOPE VALLEY - CARFRAEMILL

This 13³/₄ mile/22km in/out linear walk into the Lammermuirs' western quarter reveals, in the higher and steeper features of the range, sights seldom seen by the motorised majority as they scamper along the A68(T) over Soutra Hill. Solitude encases the walker for this grade 3 walk, with a total height gain of 1175ft/358m to the heathery summit of Lammer Law. Walking is by way of winding valley lanes and grassy paths on ancient

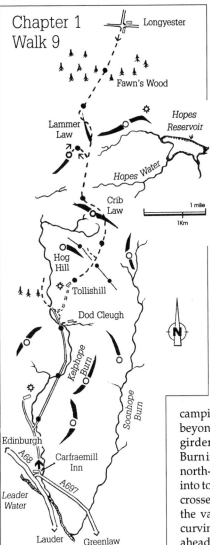

Chapter 1
Walk 9

Longyester

Fawn's Wood

Lammer
Law

Hopes
Reservoir

Hopes Water

Crib
Law

1 mile

1Km

Hog
Hill

Tollishill

Dod Cleugh

Kelphope Burn

Soonhope Burn

N

Edinburgh

Carfraemill
Inn

A68

A697

Leader
Water

Lauder   Greenlaw

rights of way over heathery fells. In winter or adverse weather, hill-walking boots/ shoes and equipment are recommended for this enjoyable 7 hour hike. The way also provides two alternative walks, A) a linear journey of 9¾ miles/15.6km, by continuing on the Right of Way to Longyester; or B) an 8 mile/12.8km linear walk from Longyester to Lammer Law, Crib Law and return.

ROUTE DIRECTIONS

Close by the junction of the A697 and A68(T), an unclassified road runs north behind Carfraemill Inn, GR 508534, giving access to Kelphope valley. Do not park in the inn car park without permission.

Start north from the inn on the country lane, past the caravan and camping site, and ³/₄ mile / 1.2km beyond the inn fork right over a girder bridge. With Kelphope Burn initially below and left, walk north-north-east along the lane into total seclusion. The lane later crosses over Kelphope Burn as the valley is narrowed by three curving bastions to the east and ahead the mounds of Tollishill (1) and Hog Hill. At lower levels grain and root crops prosper, but on the steep slopes above the thin grass dense bracken and occasional despairing silver birch and rowan support little more than pheasants, a few sheep and many rabbits.

At the junction below Dod Cleugh swing left for $^{1}/_{2}$ mile/0.8km over the flat lands below Tollishill. A grass path leaves the road for a short distance before joining the roadway rising east and north-east to the steading of Tollishill, where, by the standing stone, the public road ends and the signposted public right of way (2) to Haddington via Longyester begins.

The gradual crescent of ascent to Crib Law is via a wide track north-east and north, over stiles and under the national grid pylons, via the south-eastern flank. Prior to and beyond the pylon line at a gate, V-shaped gouges with a 'rig and furrow' appearance can be seen on either side of the track; could they have been formed by continuous lines of packhorses centuries ago? The way now passes, via a stile and gated fence, 200yds/m east from the summit of Crib Law 1670ft/509m (3) as it swings initially north-west, by Criblaw Scars for $1^{1}/_{2}$ miles/2.4km to Lammer Law. To the right the path is eaten into by these unstable scars and cleughs caused by water rushing into the wetlands surrounding Rushy Grain below.

The rounded dome of Lammer Law 1729ft/527m, to the north, is reached with ease by taking the right fork of the public path then at a slip rail, with noticeboard, turn left with the wide track leading north-west to the large 'cairn' topping this grandstand of a summit (3).

Return to the slip rail, turn right and with the outward route via Tollishill and Kelphope descend to Carfraemill.

ALTERNATIVE WALKS:
A) From Lammer Law the way continues north and north-north-east for $2^{3}/_{4}$ miles/4.4km to Longyester, descending steadily and offering fine views over East Lothian. The walk first follows heather-clad fells, then as height is lost at the approaches to Blinkbonny and Fawn's Wood it takes the straight white road to Longyester.
B) From Longyester, where parking may be difficult, to Crib Law and back. A pleasing, rewarding and steady walk that if desired takes in the summit of Lammer Law. Best undertaken on a clear day

in order to appreciate the extensive views.

Accommodation and refreshments at Carfraemill, Oxton and Gifford.

ITEMS OF INTEREST ALONG THE WAY

(1) TOLLISHILL. An Iron Age fort caps the summit of Tollishill and a solitary Standing Stone remains by the farm, but the fame of Tollishill lies in the old proverb "Ilka bannock had its maike (equal) but the bannock o' Tollishill". The bannocks were unequalled because they were baked with gold in their centres and conveyed via John, Duke of Lauderdale, to Charles II. These priceless bannocks were baked by Margaret Lylestone, 'Midside Maggie', wife of the tenant of Tollishill and taken by her to Tollishill's laird, the Duke of Lauderdale.

(2) LAUDER TO HADDINGTON WAY. A medieval route across the high Lammermuirs, ascending Tollishill by the Standing Stone to the upper reaches of Crib Law and Lammer Law, before descending to Longyester and Haddinton. A way used by merchants and cadgers, with wool from Lauderdale as the main commodity carried north and grain from the fertile acres of East Lothian for the return journey. A way also used as a local drove road.

(3) CRIB LAW & LAMMER LAW. As examples of classic mountain form they have little to offer; as grandstands and providers of views they are of the first rank. They provide immediate views of Lauderdale, the Lothian's coastal plain and Edinburgh, with its plume of Pentland Hills streaming south-west. More distant is the Firth of Forth lapping the Kingdom of Fife, and in the hazy distance the Perthshire highlands. Over the heather-clad Lammermuir plateau, flat save for an occasional pimpled top or crevassed by a meltwater channel, can be seen the bountiful Tweed valley, its patchwork ringed by the border bastions of the Cheviots, Ettrick Forest and the Tweedsmuir Hills.

WALK 10: "Via Trita, Via Tuta" (2)

CHANNELKIRK - ROMAN CAMP - DERE STREET - KING'S INCH - SOUTRA AISLE

A 4 mile/6.4km tramp ascending 328ft/100m on the Roman road of Dere Street, high above the muted bustle of the A68(T), to the Red Monks sanctuary on Soutra Hill. Graded 2 this 2¹/₂ hour route over country lanes, farm tracks, and faint fell paths calls for walking boots and hill-walking clothing. A walk of interest and appreciation.

ROUTE DIRECTIONS

West of the busy A68(T), ¹/₂ mile/0.8km north of the Carfraemill roundabout, a signposted minor road leads immediately into the village of Oxton. Turn right at the Tower Hotel, ie. north, for 1¹/₂ miles/2.4km to the signposted church at Channelkirk, GR 482545. Limited car parking is available opposite the church entrance; please do not obstruct parking for those attending Sunday 10am services.

The church is our starting point, but is itself of interest and the kirkyard provides fine introductory views of Lauderdale. Walk west on the tree-lined angled farm road, passing several houses and a noisy rookery, 'a Craw's waddin'. Fork right at Kirktonhill farmhouse then turn sharp right at its cottage onto a cart track northwards, alongside a plantation, to the remains of a Roman encampment (1) on the right. Ahead the distinct profile of Dere Street (2) can be seen spearing north, between the steep sided gully of Raugby Burn and the hump of Turf Law. Two gates in the stone walls lead past Roman earthworks, ie. east of the northbound wall, from where the raised way of Dere Street is marked by an interpretive sign.

This Roman lifeline provides 3 exhilarating miles/4.8km of fell walking in the grand manner. Unfortunately an encroaching Sitka stand has buried 1 mile/0.8km of the central section, forcing the walker off the Street's well-drained bed onto the stand's eastern fringes on a rush infested gated way. The Street is rejoined before descending to the gap at Kings' Inch (3) below Dun Law. Cross boggy Armet Water by the right-hand trees, and ascend right, over an upland pasture, for a marker sign and the B6368 a few yds/m

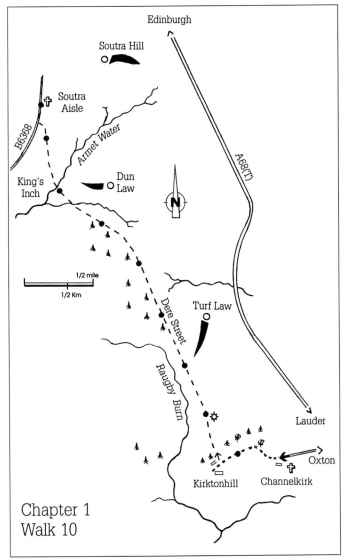

Chapter 1
Walk 10

south of the hospice at Soutra Aisle (4). Do not hurry from this unique place.

A return to Channelkirk by the outward route is equally pleasing should transport be unavailable.

Accommodation and refreshments available in Oxton and Carfraemill.

ITEMS OF INTEREST ALONG THE WAY

(1) CHANNELKIRK. A Roman station above Kirktonhill at the head of Lauderdale on the great pass of Dun Law and Soutra Hill, linked to the camps of Trimontium (Melrose) to the south and Inveresk and the Antonine Wall to the north by the thoroughfare of Dere Street.

(2) DERE STREET. "The beaten path is the safe path"; a raised ridge with a convex surface, 7yds/m wide and flanked by ditches that provided surface hard core and when cleared, drainage. It was built at the instigation of Governor Julius Agricola around AD 80, as one of the main northern arteries through Roman Britain; a road that stretched from Tees to Tyne before battling north through wild and inhospitable Border terrain to the Lothian plains and the Firth of Forth. Its route into Lauderdale via King's Inch, the highest since the Cheviots, to the sanctuary of Soutra Aisle has been traced and signposted. It is a 1900-year-old memorial to the skills of Roman military engineers and the sweat of slave labour.

(3) KING'S INCH. This junction of Dere Street and the ancient ecclesiastical way known as Girthgate - Malcolm's Rode, has been described as "a rendezvous for gypsies and vagrants" and was much used by generations of drovers as a resting place.

(4) SOUTRA AISLE. The 'Domus Soltre' of the Red or Trinity Friars, founded at Soltre (Soutra Hill) in 1184 by Malcolm I of Scotland. It grew in stature as a sanctuary and a place of succour for those who journeyed in this wilderness, but sadly declined after 1462 when Mary of Gueldres linked its resources to Trinity College Edinburgh. Only a small section of the original remains. The Aisle has been partially restored, with several inscribed slabs embedded in its walls.

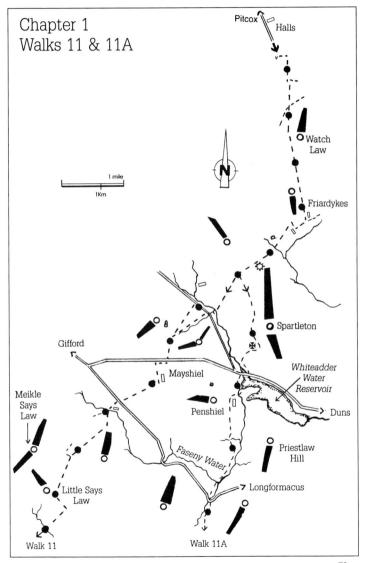

Chapter 1
Walks 11 & 11A

Pitcox

Halls

Watch Law

Friardykes

Spartleton

Whiteadder Water Reservoir

Duns

Gifford

Mayshiel

Meikle Says Law

Penshiel

Priestlaw Hill

Faseny Water

Longformacus

Little Says Law

Walk 11

Walk 11A

1 mile

1 Km

N

WALK 11: The Herring Road to Lauder

HALLS - WATCH LAW - FRIARDYKES - WHITEADDER WATER - KINGSIDE BURN - MAYSHIEL - FASENY COTTAGE - LITTLE SAYS LAW - LITTLE LAW - HUNT LAW - WEDDER LAW - LYLESTONE HILL - BURNCASTLE - NEWBIGGING WALLS GR 531503

Old Tracks, such as the Herring Road, in Berwickshire are listed as assumed rights of way.

The Herring Road as recorded by the Ordnance Survey in Parish Name books in the 1850s was listed as "A track leading from Dunbar to Lauder across the moors, mostly frequented by Drovers taking herds of Cattle and Sheep to fairs &c; formerly much used by Fish Hawkers, particularly during the Herring Season, hence its name. It was formerly used by the inhabitants of Lauderdale and others for the conveyance of Herring &c from Dunbar".

*Two ways lay claim to the name, offering the pedestrian challenging and rewarding aspects of the Lammermuirs. Both are long with possible navigational problems and as such should only be tackled as a one-day exercise by fit and experienced hill walkers. The original Herring Road route, from Dunbar to Lauder, is described in detail. A shorter alternative from Dunbar to Westruther also provides a good day's hike and is described briefly in **Walk 11A**.*

The Herring Road over the Lammermuir Hills from Lothian Edge to Lauderdale covers 20 miles/32km to Newbigging and approaching 25 miles/40km into the centre of Lauder, with a total ascent of 2264ft/690m. Graded 4 for reasons of length and navigation it involves 10 hours' walking time to Lauder. Underfoot are farm tracks, ancient grassy ways, open fell with rutted paths through heather and stretches of hard core National Grid road. The route requires navigational and map skills as no waymarks or signs are posted (with the exception of one at the starting point at Halls). Hill-walking footwear, equipment, water and rations are essential. For those wishing a shorter journey, pick-up points are the Whiteadder Water road at Kingside Burn GR 637656, the B6355 by Mayshiel GR 625646, or the Longformacus/Gifford road at Redstone Rig GR 613636. In the mid 1600s more than 20,000 pedestrians per year travelled to Dunbar - the majority on foot!

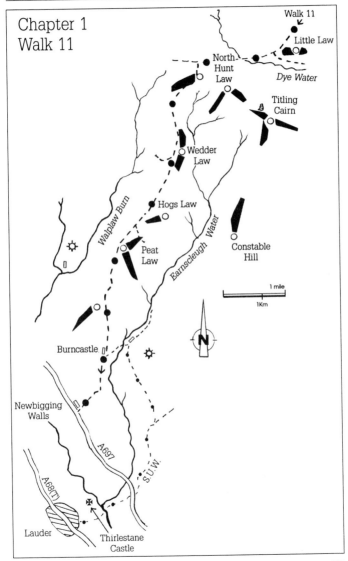

Chapter 1
Walk 11

Walk 11

Little Law

Dye Water

North Hunt Law

Titling Cairn

Wedder Law

Hogs Law

Waplaw Burn

Earnscleugh Water

Peat Law

Constable Hill

1 mile

1Km

N

Burncastle

Newbigging Walls

A697

S.U.W.

A68(T)

Lauder

Thirlestane Castle

ROUTE DIRECTIONS

The farm of Halls, GR 653727, 5 miles/8km south from the old fishing port of Dunbar, via the B6370 and a minor road from Pitcox, marks the beginning of the Herring Road (1). 600yds/554m south of Halls at the cattle grid a signpost points east and declares 'Public Path Lauder 20 miles'. Cars can be turned beyond the cattle grid, but not parked.

Follow the cart track/stone wall east for ¼ mile/0.4km, turning right at a gate, ie. south, to ascend the grass and scrub-clad flanks of Lothian Edge alongside a gorse-covered cleugh. Beyond the third gate the deep ruts of the Herring Road can be seen scarring the ascent. Leave the cart track at a rocky S-bend to climb with the deeply rutted slopes. This rutted way is the first indication of regular passage by heavy laden packhorses and carts centuries ago. Note also Dunbar and the Firth of Forth behind.

At a tracked crossroads ignore the better track through the gate and continue south to the grassy and flat summit of Watch Law. There are several V-shaped tracks (packhorse) and flat-bottomed tracks (carts) branching to the west across Dunbar Common; these ways however lead into spruce plantations with restricted passage.

A marker stone, with a suggestion of past lettering, stands at a gate on Watch Law where several tracks offer themselves. Take the right-hand one by a guiding fence, eventually descending left, ie. south. Ruts are now clearly visible underfoot on the approaches to Friardykes Dod and the somewhat derelict steading of Friardykes (2). Here a National Grid road is joined leading to the nearby and equally weary buildings of Beltondod.

The line of pylons overhead and the accompanying road slicing over Spartleton Edge do not improve the Lammermuir skyline; they do however provide a navigational aid on this otherwise featureless plateau, plus a walkable route to Whiteadder Water. This removes the problem of thrashing through tangled heather or picking a way through the conifer maze. The road passes Yadlee Cottage at the head of Bothwell Water and the site of a stone circle (not visible to the author) as it ascends Ling Rig, before descending into the pleasing haughs of Whiteadder Water (3) at the confluence of Kingside Burn with its ford and somewhat incongruous arched footbridge. Continue south-west on distinct sheep traces above the north bank of Kingside Burn, or follow the minor road north-west for 600yds/m to a bridleway leading south and then south-west through heather on Nine Stone Rig (note the Stone Circle). Both routes meet, crossing the burn at the intersection with the pylons.

Once across, more hollow tracks are visible below a conifer stand which, when passed, lead via a gate to the B6355 road; cross and strike west in a strip of trees to the driveway leading south towards the fine old house of Mayshiel. Pass the house on the right, ie. north, side from where a distinct track rises so..th-west to the source of Kell Burn and the minor road beyond as it crosses Redstone Rig. Cross the road to a gate (padlocked for vehicular restriction) leading south-west on a steeply descending stony road to Faseny Cottage by Faseny Burn - no building was shown on the 6-inch OS map of 1853. This lonely secluded glen, where visual evidence of the Herring Road is sparse, is crossed at the ford taking the left, ie. most southerly, of the moorland tracks across Little Collar Law, rising south and south-west and south for $1^{1}/_{2}$ miles/ 2.4km to Little Says Law 1569ft/478m, a flat and characterless top by the county fence of Berwickshire and East Lothian. This site no doubt inspired a hapless traveller to describe the Lammermuirs as "sterile and heath-clad blackness".

Ahead, from Little Says Law to the barely distinguishable North Hart Law 1591ft/485m, the highest point en route, little remains of the ruts of the Herring Road. As Little Says Law is not a place to linger, veer left, ie. south-east, and south by the heather-bound fence for 1 mile, leaving it as it angles sharply east above Black Burn, running into 'Burn Betwixt the Laws' (ie. Meikle Law and Little Law). Descend south over the rough terrain, parallel with the burns, for $^{1}/_{4}$ mile/400m to join the wide walkway of the pylon road, then right for $^{1}/_{2}$ mile/0.8km south-west to the foot of Little Law, where a road enters from the left. A few yards down this road lies Shiel, GR 587590, an old inn now derelict but no doubt a welcome halt for the Fish-Cadger (5) of old.

There is little doubt that the Herring Road travelled from Shiel south-west along one of the feeder burns, rising to Hunt Law and North Hart Law. Today this route is rough underfoot, therefore for ease of passage return to the pylon road, ascending west for $1^{1}/_{4}$ miles/2km to a cattle grid, gate and District boundary fence. Swing left with the fence for 400yds/m on a swiped path to the gated top of North Hart Law.

From North Hart Law a distinct grass and dirt bridleway rides the ridge top, south-west and south, for 5 exhilarating miles/8km to Burncastle, passing en route the descriptive tops of Wedder Law, Hogs Law, Peat Law and Lylestone Law high above the winding glens of Whalplaw and Earnscleugh, green with bracken and purple with heather. As Burncastle is approached the picturesque floor of Lauderdale and the Moorfoot hills please the eye. From Burncastle steading descend to the busy A697 at Newbigging Walls, where hopefully a prearranged lift awaits as the A697 is not walker friendly. Should transport not be available, walk south with the A697 for 1³/₄ miles/2.8km to the waymarked (a thistle) Southern Upland Way at Wanton Walls road end. Turn right and follow the waymarks for the final yards into Lauder.

Welcome accommodation and refreshments in Lauder.

ITEMS OF INTEREST ALONG THE WAY

(1) THE HERRING ROAD. What remains of the road today, for much has been buried by the plough, tells us a great deal about who and what travelled across the lonely fells of Lammermuir. The deep gouged V-shaped tracks clearly reflect the passage of packhorses, whereas the use of heavy laden carts can be traced by two shallow ruts with a flat-bottomed track between. As with all moorland roads the Herring Road favoured the higher ground, ascent and descent being less of a problem on the drier and harder ground than on the lower and wetter areas.

WHO USED THE HERRING ROAD? In 1651 the confluence of people at Dunbar to the herring-fishery amounted to 20,000 persons buying the cured and barrelled-up herring. In the eighteenth century the good folk of Westruther used to provide a sort of seasoning to their bread by laying in a stock of herrings at Lammas, going in bands to Dunbar and making purchases of as many fish as would serve their families during winter. The parish of Lauder also mentions the Road in the Kirk Session record, chastising a parishioner for "going to the herring upon Sabbeth day".

In addition to the herring trade, the way was used by packmen and itinerant traders who serviced the isolated villages and outlying farms. A dash of romanticism is supplied by the 18th century smugglers from the coasts of Berwickshire and Northumberland, who ran their brandy and claret not only to tower, farm and manse but also to the inns at Danskine and possibly Shiel. The military also left their mark on sections of the route by Whiteadder Water, transporting masses of animals and ordnance - 17 cannon weighing 4000lbs, drawn by teams totalling 450 oxen.

(2) FRIARDYKES. The name of this isolated shepherd's cottage is derived from a medieval settlement for wayward monks. Under the auspices of Melrose Abbey back-sliders were sent to these desolate moors to consider their misdeeds and failings before returning, hopefully chastened, to the tranquillity of Tweeddale. Sadly this centre of repentance was subjected to unacceptable pressures when a nunnery was established on a nearby height. The nuns, to ease the repentants' apparent burdens, showed them little kindnesses, which sadly only exacerbated the problems and caused the monks to depart, never to return.

(3) WELLS. Several wells of crystal clear water spring to life close by or within walking distance of the Herring Road, such as Davie's Well below Friardykes Dod and White Well, GR 619676, by Whiteadder Water. These wells were known as 'Verter or Virtue' wells, for when their crystal cold waters pass your lips, "the hills will share their secrets with you and the streams begin to babble with a more articulate voice". The author can vouch for the quality of the water; as to the latter it is for the reader to judge.

(4) SHIEL INN. The name of this old inn is uncertain and several versions exist as to its exact whereabouts, though the site at Shiel is documented. It states that an innkeeper of the Shiel Inn by Dye Water, one Margaret Dunhome, was burnt as a witch in the 17th century.

(5) FISH-CADGERS or CADDIES. Carriers who purchased herring at Dunbar and distributed and sold the 'Silver Darlings' inland are documented in the early 1800s. The fish was transported in baskets slung from teams of packhorses who walked in single file, the lead horse wearing a bell to guide those following.

WALK 11A: The Herring Road to Westruther

HALLS GR 653727 - WATCH LAW - FRIARDYKES DOD - SPARTLETON - GAMELSHIEL CASTLE - PENSHIEL - KILLPALLET FORD - TROTTINGSHAW - SCAR LAW - WEDDERLIE - WESTRUTHER GR 634500

The total distance is 18¹/₂ miles/29.6km with ascents of 2291ft/698m, the highest point being 1350ft/411m. Graded 4, the journey involves 8/8¹/₂ hours' walking time. This route exhibits more visible evidence of the passage of fish-laden packhorses and carts than **Walk 11**, *with perhaps better tracks and paths underfoot. The surrounding scenery is also more varied and pleasing on the eye. This walk still remains a major undertaking: wear the appropriate gear for the conditions and carry map, compass, guidebook, water and provisions.*

ROUTE DIRECTIONS

The directions are as in **Walk 11** from Halls to Ling Rig, GR 645668, where the fence crosses the pylon road. Turn left, ie. south-east, with the fence on Ling Rig. The pathway then leaves the fence for a pleasing picturesque descent via the ruins of Gamelshiel Castle and the north flank of Summer Hill to the shimmering waters of Whiteadder reservoir. The reservoir is turned at its north-west end taking the farm road by Penshiel south, passing the ruins of Penshiel Grange and Chapel Stone (standing stone) to cross Faseny Water and Killpallet Burn.

As the Longformacus to Gifford road is crossed, and the way ascends south above Killpallet, the telltale signs of packhorse passage can be seen as we progress over the expanse of Lamb Hill and descend to Trottingshaw in the Dye valley. The Road continues south, laboriously clambering out of Dye Water over Scar Law, to briefly flirt with the Southern Upland Way west of Watch Water and east of Twin Law. This section offers the finest of views across the Tweed valley to the Border line of the Cheviot Hills.

Scar Law marks a walking watershed, for it is mainly downhill in a southerly direction for the remaining 4 miles/6.4km passing Cralaw and Wedderlie to meet the B6456, with Westruther to the right, ie. west.

Accommodation and refreshment at the Thistle, Westruther.

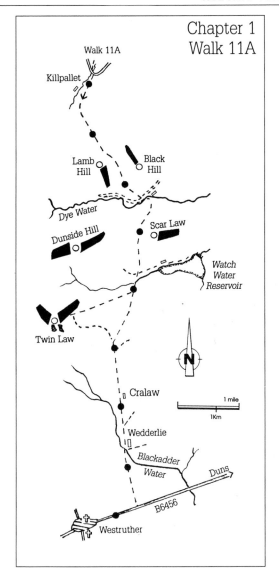

Chapter 1
Walk 11A

Walk 11A

Killpallet

Lamb Hill

Black Hill

Dye Water

Dunside Hill

Scar Law

Watch Water Reservoir

Twin Law

Cralaw

Wedderlie

Blackadder Water

Duns

B6456

Westruther

1 mile

1Km

N

CHAPTER 2
Moorfoot Hills

By glen and streamlet winded still,
Where stunted birches hid the rill,
Sir Walter Scott, *Marmion*

THE AREA

A range of hills distinguished enough to warrant their own name for at least 1500 years and to be recorded 800 years ago in the 'Registrum de Neubotle' or cartulary of Newbattle Abbey; founded by David I in the 12th century. Reference is made to 'Morthwait', an adjoining wasteland or forest near the source of the South Esk by the two mountains known today as Bowbeat Hill and Blackhope Scar. The name, given no doubt by earlier Norse settlers, incorporates the Scandinavian word *thveit* - a clearing, and designates the area we know now as the Moorfoots.

The Moorfoots were almost entirely pastoral, though today much of the southern and western quadrant is given over to forestry. The range exceeds 1500ft/457m in the main, yet fails to exceed 2162ft/659m, with a mere five mountains topping 2000ft/610m. From such statistics one would imagine a flat plateau, such as is seen in the Lammermuirs, but this is not the case for a host of distinct summits, domed and isolated, crowd around the shoulders of the highest hills; divided yet connected by interwining steep sided ridges and wild pensive glens. Fine of form in the Border mould, there is an absence of nakedness that gives the Moorfoots a softer appeal. A mystical remoteness of hills unexplored, where the gentle brooding melancholy lifts as the morning mists when the summit is conquered and the range revealed.

The highest hills, with one notable exception, are grouped in the western Moorfoots, where only the tops of Jeffries Corse, Dundreich, Bowbeat Hill, Blackhope Scar, Garvald Punks and Whitehope Law exceed 2000ft/610m, although several attractive adjoining hills

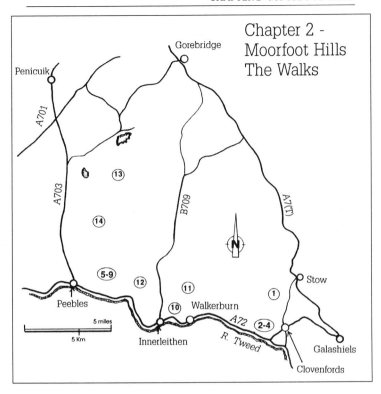

Chapter 2 -
Moorfoot Hills
The Walks

approach mountain height. To the east of Leithen Water, high above the Tweed, stands Windlestraw Law, the highest of all at 2162ft/ 659m. The remainder decrease in height as they slope north and east, where many of the higher ridges and plateaux are wet and 'clatchy' underfoot, often split by steep sided gullies, such as Wolf Cleugh, Glentress Burn and upper Caddon Water, the conduits of flash floods and raging spates.

Confined between the Tweed valley and the Lothian plain and hemmed in by the Lammermuirs to the east and the Cloich Hills to the west, the entire range is but 13 miles / 20.8km from north to south and 14 miles / 22.4km from east to west. Such compression minimises

Whitehope Farm and Whitehope Law

the walk-in and walk-out distances, and allows immediate access to the higher fells. The northern boundary, an immediate and conspicuous rim, is a continuation of the Lammermuir fault line that delineates the divide of the Southern Uplands and the Central Lowlands; whilst the eastern perimeter is neatly marked by Gala Water and the A7 road. The picturesque Tweed valley, through which the A72 winds, marks the southern marches; with an equally steep western flank running with Eddleston Water and the A703, neatly packaging these compact hills. A parcel secured by Galashiels and Peebles at the south-east and south-west corners, with the capital, Edinburgh, a mere 13 miles/21km north from Fala Hill.

Unlike many of the Southern Upland ranges the Moorfoots are bisected north and south by road, the B709 and B7007, and river. Roads that rise and fall with Heriot Water, Dewar Water, a connecting glacial breach, Glentress Water and Leithen Water. A narrow and tortuous passage, lined with crumbling keeps and towers, that was much used centuries ago; whose highest point at Windy Slack rises to 1320ft/402m, 128ft/39m higher than the A68 crossing Soutra Hill.

Distinguishing landmarks, distinctive peaks and definitive footpaths are, in places, somewhat thin on the ground, making navigation and progress a hazardous pursuit in adverse weather conditions. An average rainfall of 40 inches per year on high ground and $34^{1/2}$ inches in the valleys may seem, for an upland area, slight. It is nevertheless enough to more than top up the spongy water-table on the high plateaux, where passage, over Garvold Punks for example, can be tedious and in places reduced to a dangerous crawl through trenches of glutinous peat. It is just below the Punks, at the track summit north from Glentress Water, that marks the site of the Piper's Grave; a piper who was attempting to play his pipes continuously from Peebles to Lauder expired at this spot. Fortunately many traversing ridges have navigational aids in the form of boundary fences and dykes, and also relatively dry paths and tracks underfoot. These ways have been accessed and walked for generations, thanks to considerate understandings between landowners and walkers.

Accommodation and refreshments are available, at inns, bed and breakfasts and campsites scattered around the perimeter of the range. From the north in a clockwise direction - Gorebridge, Middleton, Stow, Galashiels, Clovenfords, Walkerburn, Innerleithen, Peebles, Eddleston and Leadburn. The nearest youth hostels are at Edinburgh and Melrose.

Public transport runs from:

Edinburgh to	-	Stow and Galashiels. Leadburn, Eddleston and Peebles
Galashiels to	-	Clovenfords, Walkerburn, Innerleithen, Glentress, Peebles
Moffat and Biggar to	-	Peebles

Timetables available at bus stations and tourist information centres.

THE WALKS

Maps: OS Landranger Series 1:50,000, Sheet 73.
         OS Pathfinder 1:25,000, 434, 448, 449, 460, 461.
         Forest Enterprise, Forests of the Tweed Valley.

Walk 1, though linear, is a practical and visual introduction to the Moorfoots; as is Walk 2 to the many Moorfoot forest trails. Walks 3 and 4 continue with the forest theme in Thornylee with enticing views against the silhouettes of further walks. Walks 5 to 8 visit and explore the coniferous cloak of Glentress Forest as it enshrouds the steep sided valleys and soft topped hills above the silvery Tweed: four stimulating waymarked walks that periodically break out of the trees to provide extensive views of this intriguing countryside.

Walk 9, although still in Glentress Forest, ventures just that bit higher and longer for those extra special views that make a good walk great; whilst Walk 10 provides a testing taster as it approaches the most southerly and highest Donald in the Moorfoots. Walk 11 ascends that mountain, Windlestraw Law, on a demanding walk-in; the summit and the ridge descent are visually stimulating. Walks 12 and 12A, both linear, ascend the most pleasing of the Moorfoot Hills, Lee Pen, as a starter for one of the finest ridge walks to Peebles. Walk 13 horseshoes high around the cirque of the South Esk. Finally Walk 14, a high-level trek, recalls our lost youth as it traverses 14 miles/22.4km over 11 tops, never lower than 1500ft/457m nor higher than 2041ft/622m; can you imagine the exhilaration?

INFORMATION TABLE

WALK	DISTANCE Miles/Kilometres		ASCENT Feet/Metres		D of D *	TIME Hours
1	12½	20	1148	350	3	5½
2	1½	2.5	328	100	1	1
3	2½	4	656	200	2	1½
4	3¼	5	820	250	2	2¼
5	3	4.8	640	195	2	1¾
6	6	9.6	1253	382	2½	3½
7	4½	7.2	574	175	2	2¾
8	2¼	3.6	427	130	1	1¼
9	9½	15.2	1893	577	3	5
10	7	11.2	1706	520	3	4
11	12	19.2	2323	708	3	6/7
12	11	17.6	2316	706	3	6/7
12A	9½	15.2	2152	656	3	5
13	10½	16.8	1778	542	3	5½
14	14	22.4	2893	882	4	7½

*Degree of Difficulty
1 - Good path, no appreciable ascent, no navigational problems.
2 - Distinct paths, noticeable ascents, longer walk.
3 - Paths rough or indistinct, ascent demanding, navigation required
4 - Walk long, demanding compass and mountain skills, high exposure.

WALK 1: Caddon Water

STOW - LUGATE WATER - THE LODGE - SCROOF - CADDON
WATER - CRAIG HEAD - BLACKHAUGH - CLOVENFORDS

*From Stow on Gala Water, via Caddon Water, to the valley of the Tweed
this agreeable linear walk probes 12¹/₂ miles/20km through the southern
foothills of the Moorfoot range. Graded 3, the route treads country lanes,
tracks and fell paths through steep sided glens and over fine open ridges,
ascending a total of 1148ft/350m. Walking boots/shoes and comfortable
clothing to match the conditions should be worn for this scenic taster of
5¹/₂ hours. A walk rich in wildlife, particularly birds and mountain hares.
It is advisable when crossing the grouse moors of Scroof and Dunlee during
the spring nesting season to keep at all times to the pathway, and to avoid
the area during the shooting season.*

ROUTE DIRECTIONS
Stow, a small township in the historic and scenically pleasing valley
of Gala Water (1), straddles the A7 at GR 459456, our starting point
for this walk.

From the crossroads at the southern end walk west to cross Gala
Water, ascending by the old Waverley line to fork left onto the road
south. The remains of the old 'Collection' bridge over Gala Water
can be seen below the church. 1 mile/1.6km from Stow, Lugate
Water is crossed via a three-arched stone bridge, then it's immediately
right to Lugate Farm. At the farm fork swing left through the
steading to a wood-walled bungalow, where the right fork is taken
north-west on a hard road above Lugate Water (2). Solitude and
bird calls provide company over Fowie Rig, before turning left by
Fowie Burn to the washed walls of The Lodge.

Keep left at The Lodge fork, winding with the burn to leave the
track at its obtuse angle below Fowie. Continue west, on the north
side of Back Burn, ascending via a bridleway for 433yds/400m to
the 985ft/300m contour line. At this point the burn swings left and
we continue west to the narrow L-shaped coniferous plantation
above. Pass through a gap in this shelter belt, just north of the
angled-L, to emerge onto a twin track below the flat top of Hard
Law, leading west over grass and heather on North Rig to the
cairned and heather-clad col between Dunlee Hill and Scroof Hill.

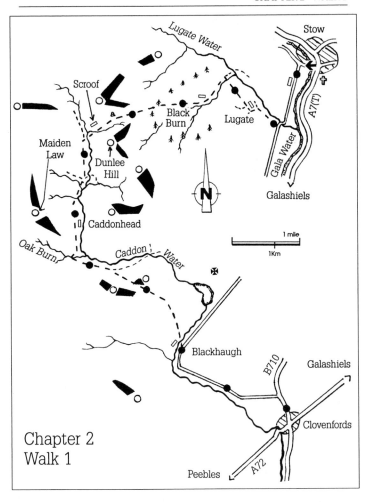

The energy expended during the 590ft/180m ascent from Back Burn is instantly replaced by the Moorfoot views (3) ahead. Pass through the slip rail and descend south-west, on a narrow path through managed heather north of Scroof Burn, to the half hidden

89

shieling of Scroof, with its nearby Moses's Well.

From Scroof a farm track winds south into the ever changing light of Caddon Water glen (4), following the bowed-banks of Caddon below the skirts of Great Law and Maiden Law to the crouched buildings of Caddonhead Farm. Continue south by road, crossing Oak Burn, to swing left around the steep slopes of Nether Hill to a fork in the farm track. Take the right fork of this grided and gated road, rising to the col between Craig Head and Black Law, a section that provides views of the Tweed valley and Minch Moor ridge. Caddon Water is rejoined at Blackhaugh by descending south-east and south for $1^{1}/_{2}$ miles/2.4km; from here a country lane passes Newhall, Graiglatch and Whytbank to meet the B710, $^{1}/_{2}$ mile/0.8km above Clovenfords (5): nob't a downhill stroll to journey's end.

Accommodation and refreshments at Clovenfords and nearby Galashiels.

ITEMS OF INTEREST ALONG THE WAY

(1) GALA WATER. Known in ancient times as Wedale/Waedale, the dale of sorrow or woe, and sight of the bloody battle of Guinnion, one of twelve fought by the legendary King Arthur. A dale that was the haunt of reiving families: one such was the Hoppringles or Pringles, and above Stow there is a stone, now embedded in a farmhouse wall, bearing the inscription "I.P.M.P. In Te Domine Spevari. 1626".

(2) LUGATE WATER. Or by its ancient name, Ewes Water, it was once home to otters. This principal tributary to Gala Water is subject to flash floods and violent spates. In 1735 an incessant deluge caused the face of Weather Law, above Over Shiels on Lugate Water, to slip and slide with the raging torrents, drowning sheep and washing enough peats down to Galashiels "as to provide the inhabitants with a winter's fuel".

((3) MOORFOOT VIEWS. Due west the hog's back of Windlestraw Law, rising from Seathope Law and Maiden Law, continues north-west over the sterile ridge of Pringles Green and Eastside Heights to the steep sided glacial fault of Glentress and Dewar.

(4) CADDON WATER. Whose source seeps from Caddon Head,

north of Windlestraw Law, for many picturesque miles to the Tweed at Caddonfoot. Three peles, Blackhaugh, Red Doors and Windydoors, stood on its braes; only Windydoors has withstood the military and farmhouse builders.

(5) CLOVENFORDS. Originally called Whytbank Lea, this village was a coaching stop on the Tweeddale route from Edinburgh. The coaching inn, which remains today, provided lodgings for Sir Walter Scott prior to his moving into nearby Ashiestiel; where he wrote *The Lady of the Lake and Marmion*. Wordsworth called in 1803, in *Yarrow Revisited:* "And with the Tweed had travelled, and when we came to Clovenfords".

WALKS 2 to 8: Moorfoot Forest Trails

THORNYLEE FOREST - WALKS 2 to 4 FROM THORNYLEE CAR PARK & PICNIC PLACE, GR 407365
GLENTRESS FOREST - WALKS 5 to 8 FROM FALLA BRAE CAR PARK & PICNIC PLACE, GR 287403

The Foresty Commission's holdings (1) of Glentress, the oldest in southern Scotland, and Thornylee rise from the banks of the Tweed and the A72 on the southern flanks of the Moorfoot Hills, providing for the walker a network of pleasing circular walks that can be as strenuous or as easy as the walker wishes, either by choosing an appropriate waymarked trail or by combining or reducing individual walks. No matter which method you choose, all walks have one virtue in common: the interest factor is always high. Information pamphlets and a Wayfaring Pack are available from Forest Enterprise, Greenside, Peebles; Falla Brae, Glentress Forest; Peebles Tourist Information Centre and local tourist information points.

Thornylee, a small forest east of Glentress with a pleasing mix of trees, rises to 1247ft/380m above the Tweed. Three waymarked colour-coded routes, with viewpoints, range from easy to moderate grades and provide the walker with many fine and ever changing prospects of Tweeddale and its rumbustuous past (2).

Glentress, the larger forest, clothes a considerable area of the watershed running south from Dundreich to the extinct volcano of Lee Pen above Innerleithen. A jigsaw of steep-sided domed hills and encroaching gullies

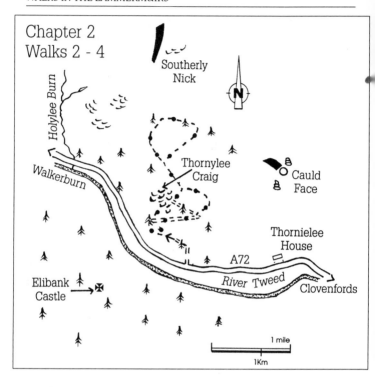

and glens provides four waymarked (colour-coded) walks, varying from short and easy to longer, steeper and strenuous.

THORNYLEE
ROUTE DIRECTIONS

A car park and picnic place, fringed with silver birch, overlooks the A72 from the north 4 miles / 6.4km west of Clovenfords and 4 miles / 6.4km east from Walkerburn, where a noticeboard, marking the starting / finishing point, gives basic details of routes, distances and colour codes for all three walks.

WALK 2: Coded yellow - 1¹/₂ miles / 2.5km, height gain 328ft / 100m and graded 1. Start on the grassy path north, via three steps, to gently ascend the zigzag figure-of-eight route in an anti-clockwise direction. A most pleasant stroll, on waymarked forest tracks and paths with seats and picnic tables along the way, offering fine views of Tweeddale and the surrounding hills and in particular the ruins of Elibank Castle (2).

WALK 3: Coded blue - Graded 2, covering $1^1/2$ miles/4km with a height gain of 656ft/200m, this walk rises well above the valley floor as it utilises the yellow-coded route, only to leave the yellow waymarks at their highest point to continue north with the forest track to the waymarked pond (3) (a few yards right of the path); the waymarks on this stretch only carry blue and red. Continue rising to a T-junction, turn left, ie. west, and 30yds/m ahead note the moss-covered stones of a circular Stone Age burial cairn hiding amongst the trees on the right. At the next junction ascend right, on a narrow heathery path with the forest ride, to a viewpoint, picnic bench and crumbling cairn. An open area offers sightings of forest raptors, the cairned Cauld Face and the winding Tweed beyond Thornylee. Return via the route of ascent to the point where **Walk 2** was left, and at the three-coloured waymark plunge right into the larch for a steep return to the car park.

WALK 4: Coded red - a Grade 2, $3^1/4$ miles/5km circuit ascending 820ft/250m, this most revealing walk starts west past the noticeboard via a gorse-lined grass path; swing right up the steps onto a cleared area at a road junction. Ahead, take the left forked path north as it rises steeply on over stones, roots and grass, through a boulder-strewn larch stand. The waymarked, seated way (ignore the white arrowheads) winds north to join a forest track. Turn left and trek as with blue Walk 3 to the viewpoint and picnic bench high above.

From there continue north for the final yards, via what appears to be a landscaped section of the forest with a good mix of larch, pine and spruce, to the perimeter stone wall and fence. Turn left with the narrow path, running west between conifers and dyke, rising slightly and revealing to the north-east an open undulating ridge surging to the hog's back of Windlestraw Law and the ridge of Cairn Hill, **Walk 11**, on the skyline. A stone dyke leads along the ridge, over Southerly Nick, Stony Knowe and Seathope Law to Windle-straw Law; a route that tempts, but unfortunately is not shown on the OS map as a public bridleway or path.

Leave the wall at the red waymark, descending south through tree-lined heather, a short stretch that provides one of the most pleasing views in Tweeddale. The silvery Tweed to Walkerburn and Innerleithen with the hills on either side gives the impression that one is in a mountainous area; although the height is not great the rock-strewn form is fine. At the waymarked junction that completes the red loop continue desending east by the ever present mole-hills, ignoring an incoming path on the right, to clear the trees, including the newly planted beech on the left at the walled eastern perimeter.

Turn right on a thin grassy path that descends by wall and forsaken shieling to meet the angled track and picnic place of the yellow-coded **Walk 2**. Swing right onto a sloping track that zigzags back to the car park at journey's end.

Accommodation, refreshments available in Innerleithen and Clovenfords.

GLENTRESS
ROUTE DIRECTIONS
2$^{1}/_{2}$ miles/4km east of Peebles and 4$^{3}/_{4}$ miles/7.6km north-west from Innerleithen, on the A72, a minor road leads north to Glentress and its car park, Falla Brae GR 287403.

WALK 5: Kirn Law

A favourite of mine, it covers 3 miles/4.8km as it rises and falls 640ft/195m in 1$^{3}/_{4}$ hours to and from the top of Kirn Law. This orange route, by pond (3), path and forest road, shares the start with the black 'hard men's' trail, leaving it to travel south as it ascends and contours Kirn Law. Not the most eye-catching hill, but certainly one that offers an explosion of Tweeddale panoramas. The return is steep, dramatic and pleasing as it plunges by forest paths with Cramb Burn to the ponds and Falla Brae.

WALK 6: Glentress Circuit

An adventure of 6 miles/9.6km, rising 1253ft/382m on forest roads, prepared paths and in places slithery sections of naked earth. Its 'strenuous' grading is justified by the steep sections that make you stop and admire the views. With its black/dark brown coded waymarks the trail starts at Falla Brae ascending north-west and

Glentress Forest Ponds

west above the ponds, through varied conifers and broadleaves (4), then via the south-west shoulder ridge leading to Caresman Hill. From here it's a steady ascent north for ¹/₂ mile/0.8km to the zenith of the trip, Dunslair Heights, with its tall communications tower. Return south and south-south-east via Caresman Hill to above Katie's Hass, at times steeply but with tantalising glimpses of the Lee Pen ridge and the rolling Border hills beyond the Tweed. Cramb Burn is then followed south-west by path and pond to Falla Brae and journey's end.

WALK 7: Caresman Hill

This red trail of 4¹/₂ miles/7.2km starts from the car park (open March to November) on the upper reaches of Glentress Burn GR 286421, gaining 574ft/175m to Caresman Hill on this walk of 2¹/₂/3 hours. The way is steep in sections as it travels east and north to the journey's apex, obliging the walker with extensive views of how things were, especially from the tiny clearing on Caresman Hill's summit. The return on this wildlife rich (5) walk is south-west and then north-east via the long shoulder above Glentress Burn.

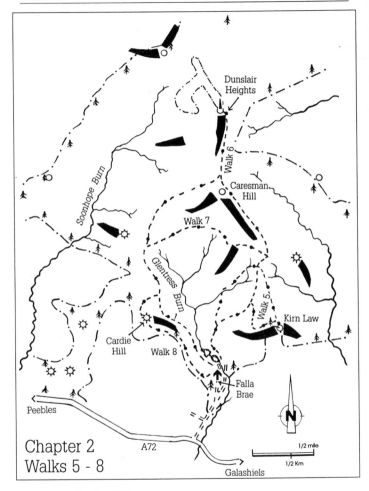

Chapter 2
Walks 5 - 8

WALK 8: Cardie Hill

This blue trail of 2¹/₄ miles / 3.6km with a height gain of 427ft / 130m, takes 1¹/₂ hours over forest roads and prepared paths. It passes the ponds, rising steadily north-west and west, before swinging south-east to the prehistoric forts on the summit of Cardie Hill. From here the path leads to a viewpoint looking over the Tweed valley to the Manor Hills beyond before returning down the shoulder of Falla Brae.

Accommodation, refreshments at Glentress, Innerleithen and Peebles.

ITEMS OF INTEREST ALONG THE WAY

(1) MOORFOOT FORESTS. Many centuries ago the Tweed valley and its surrounding hills were well wooded and formed part of the great Ettrick Forest, a much favoured hunting area for Scottish royalty up to the reign of the early Stuarts. Sadly the actions of man, by felling, charcoal burning and 'muirburning', coupled with over-grazing, particularly by sheep, destroyed the forest cover and created a vast wilderness devoid of trees. This unfortunate state has been redressed, to a certain extent, by forward-looking 19th century estate owners and later by the Forestry Commission.

(2) SHAKE LOOSE THE BORDERS. This land of legend is peppered with the visible remains of the past; prehistoric forts and settlements adorn the tops of many of the Moorfoot foothills - Cardie Hill, Horsburgh, and Pirn Craig. Later, during the killing times, pele towers rose on many a spur in Tweeddale - Woolandslee, Colquhar and, the one seen from Thornylee, Elibank. Now a ruin, gazing sightless down the Tweed, it was into its dungeons that young Will Scott of Harden was cast for attempting to reive Sir Gideon Murray's cattle. Offered the alternative, of marrying Murray's daughter Agnes, an unfortunate girl known locally as "Muckle Mou'ed Meg", or hanging by his neck till dead, Will, despite initial protestations, married Meg in 1611.

> *His hands an' his feet they bound like a sheep,*
> *An' awa' to the Elibank Tower they did hie;*
> *An' they locked him doun in a dungeon sae deep,*
> *An' they bade him prepare on the morrow to die*
>
> The Ballad of Muckle Mou'ed Meg

Will and Meg "did live happy ever after", one of their many descendants being Sir Walter Scott.

(3) FOREST PONDS. These man-made ponds support a rich mix of animals, insects and plants, including toads, frogs and spode newts; water boatmen and dragon flies; meadow sweet, water avon and

yellow flags.

(4) FOREST PRACTICE. Forest Enterprise, a part of the Forestry Commission, recognize that their vast coniferous holdings have a distinct impact on the Moorfoot and Tweeddale landscape. They are now, with the help of landscape architects, replanning and restructuring the forests, thus encouraging and providing facilities for wildlife and visitors. Spruce, once all pervading, accounts for no more than 60% of the crop; other species include larch, pine and a variety of broadleaves.

(5) FOREST WILDLIFE. In excess of 80 species of bird now inhabit the forests and their fringes, ranging from the tiny wren and colourful chaffinches to the shy grey heron, with an ever increasing count of various raptors. Nesting boxes, well above the predatory fox, can be seen in many parts of the forest, as well as bat boxes. Of the larger mammals roe deer, red squirrels, badgers and foxes are the most frequent, although mink are reputed to have colonised the cleughs and burns. Plantwise, spring and autumn present the most pleasing splashes of colour and many species of fungus provide an interesting diversion for the walker in autumn.

WALK 9: Dunslair and The Kipps

FALLA BRAE - KIRN LAW - CARESMAN HILL - DUNSLAIR
HEIGHTS - SHIELDGREEN KIPPS - CARDIE HILL - FALLA BRAE

A challenging and rewarding walk through Glentress Forest (1) ascending 1893ft/577m to the exposed viewpoints of Kirn Law, Caresman Hill, Dunslair Heights and The Kipps. Graded 3 due to the steep ascents, the route is via waymarked forest roads and paths, some grassy and peaty, onto open heathery summits. A Forest Enterprise journey of 9$^{1}/_{2}$ miles/15.2km that provides not only varied surroundings but also a pleasing habitat for the many varied flora and fauna seen along the way. Walking boots/shoes are needed, together with clothing to suit the conditions, for this 5 hour walk, and don't forget the camera.

The landscaped car park and picnic area of Falla Brae, GR 287403, with its nearby facilities including those for the not so nimble, provides the starting point. Walk north beyond the toilet

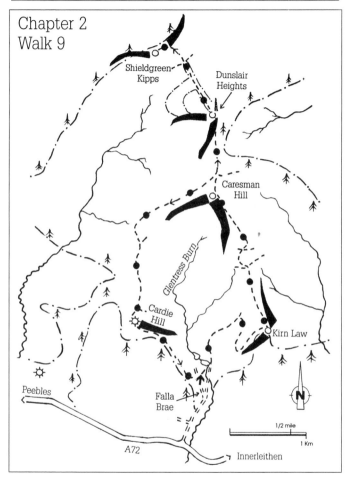

Chapter 2
Walk 9

Shieldgreen-
Kipps

Dunslair
Heights

Caresman
Hill

Glentress Burn

Cardie
Hill

Kirn Law

Peebles

Falla
Brae

N

1/2 mile

1 Km

A72

Innerleithen

cabin on the black (or is it dark brown?) colour-coded path to the ponds, teaming with feathery and fishy life. The waymarks guide the walker around the north-east fringes of the ponds then through the trees and along rising forest roads above Cramb Burn. At the second incoming road on the right an orange waymark leads onto

Pentland Hills from Shieldgreen Kipps

a dirt and grass road before plunging, almost immediately, into the left-hand trees via a narrow track for a short sharp ascent south. After ¹/₄ mile / 0.4km, at an acute angle on the route, a welcome seat by an open roadside provides fine views of Tweeddale, Cademuir (2) and Peebles. The forest, of established larch, is entered again opposite the seat, contouring north-east to a stone wall before ascending right by Scots pines to the signposted viewing platform of Kirn Law, for a graphic illustration of Tweeddale, Innerleithen, the surrounding uplands and the volcanic cone of Lee Pen.

The descent is north with the wall above the gully by Katie's Hass and Katie's Well; keep a lookout for goshawk and buzzard. At the col, black waymarks direct the walker left and then right onto the steepest path so far. On reaching the road above turn right, for 25yds/m, then left onto a rough path staggering north through conifers young and old. The waymarked route now demands effort as it continues, with a guiding stone dyke, to eventually reach the tiny clearing on Caresman Hill. It is here that exciting glimpses of the surrounding hills begin to open up, a good excuse to stop and enjoy.

From Caresman's the path continues north with dyke and ride for ¹/₂ mile/0.8km, on a more gentle ascent, finally on a hard core road, to the tower-topped summit of Dunslair Heights (3). Ahead the skyline is etched by the highland cones of Shieldgreen Kipps, our next destination, which is reached by a peaty path north by the forest's edge to the common col, then via a thin trace through tussock and heather for the final ascent to the sharp summit of the south-western Kipp. The Kipp, connected by a narrow path winding north-east and north along the forest fringes to the cones of Makeness Kipps, offers a colourful canvas of Peebles, Eddleston Water and mountain form (4).

The return to Dunslair Heights, ³/₄ mile/1.2km south, is via the outward route and from there the way is down, initially via a waymarked hard core road, first south and then south-west for 2¹/₂ miles/4km with the black coding, on road to the fork then by forest path until the crossroads at GR 278412, where the blue waymarks are met.

Turn half right onto a clearing, leaving it with the blue code south and south-east, over the treeless fort-capped summit of Cardie Hill, before descending south-east through the trees for 1 mile/1.6km on the descending shoulder of Falla Brae, with its pleasing viewpoint of Glenrath Heights beyond Glentress village, before returning to the car park and picnic area.

Accommodation, refreshments at Glentress, Innerleithen and Peebles.

ITEMS OF INTEREST ALONG THE WAY

(1) GLENTRESS FOREST. The Tweed valley, once one of the most treeless regions in Scotland, is now, thanks to farsighted 19th and 20th century landowners including Sir Walter Scott, reforested. Glentress, the oldest of Forest Enterprise's forests in southern Scotland, dating from 1920, extends from the Tweed to an elevation of 1969ft/600m, and contains spruce, larch, pine and an increasing number of hardwoods. With the trees came roe deer, red squirrels, badgers and foxes, with over 80 species of birds ranging from raptors and herons to diminutive wrens. Woodland plants flourish and fungus continues to multiply.

(2) CADEMUIR HILL. South-west of Peebles this distinct hill, scene of King Arthur's seventh battle against the pagans, stands topped

with ancient forts and dwellings. Its eastern flanks are now conifer clad.

(3) DUNSLAIR HEIGHTS 1975ft/602m. A tree-clad hill on which stands a communications tower of considerable height, no doubt to add that extra 25ft/7.6m in order to gain mountain status! The surrounds of the tower and buildings provided an experimental site for the Institute for Terrestrial Ecology, measuring the natural emission of 'greenhouse' gas - nitrous oxide - from the soil and faulted rock below.

(4) VIEWS FROM THE KIPPS. In a word, inspiring. West, across Eddlestone Water the Clioch Hills and Broughton Heights; south-west, the Tweed flanked by the dominant summit of Culter Fell, the dripping snows of Gathersnow Hill and the highest of all, Broad Law. South, the mysterious Manor valley is overlooked by Pykestone Hill, Dollar Law (hill of sorrows), Hundleshope Heights and Stob Law.

WALK 10: Windlestraw Taster

INNERLEITHEN - KIRNIE LAW - PRIESTHOPE HILL - PRIESTHOPE - PURVIS HILL - PIRN CRAIG - INNERLEITHEN

This 'taster' onto the ridges and valleys approaching Windlestraw will captivate beginner and enthusiast alike, for the circular 7 mile/11.2km route has many highlights that will please and tempt, including a rich selection of upland wildlife. Graded a mild 3, with total ascents of 1706ft/ 520m, the way is via forest roads, cart tracks, grassy paths and heathery trails as each corner turned and summit ascended reveals new and exciting views of the Moorfoots and their neighbouring ranges. Navigation on the ridges, even in poor visibility, is assisted by boundary fences and walls for a journey of 3½/4 hours. Walking boots and equipment to suit the conditions are recommended and map and compass skills will increase the visual pleasures.

ROUTE DIRECTIONS
Car parking (free) is available in Innerleithen (1) at Leithen Road north of the bridge carrying the A72. Walk north-east with the A72,

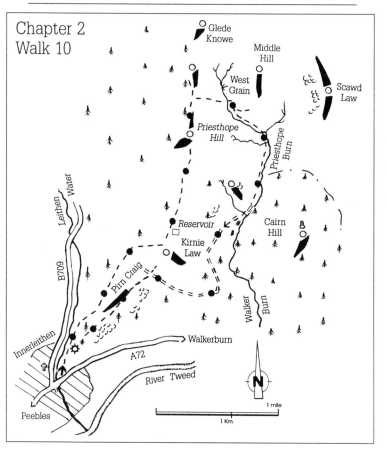

Chapter 2
Walk 10

Glede Knowe
Middle Hill
West Grain
Scawd Law
Priesthope Hill
Priesthope Burn
Leithen Water
B709
Reservoir
Kirnie Law
Cairn Hill
Pirn Craig
Walker Burn
Innerleithen
Walkerburn
A72
River Tweed
Peebles
N

1 mile
1 Km

signposted Galashiels, to Horsburgh Terrace and turn left. Pass The
Firs onto the Backs pathway, ascending to the right of an old bridge
and leading to a clearing. Ascend steeply right, by a stone dyke, to
reach a forest road, turning left at the junction. This new forest road
is followed north as far as the clearing, with views of the houses
below and the conical Lee Pen opposite. From this point it's another
section of 'huff and puff' up the forest ridge to the right to yet

another road, this time forked. Take the right fork that climbs to the broad heather-clad ridge of Kirnie Law bearing the many cubic feet of concrete that was The Reservoir (2).

From The Reservoir wind north, with one of two paths visible, ascending the gently rising flanks of Priesthope Hill followed by a rapid northerly descent between forest and fence to the col of Priesthope Sware below. At the lowest point on the col pass through a slip rail right, losing height on a narrow grassy path through bracken, to the tinkling waters of West Grain running into Priesthope Burn, which in turn becomes Walker Burn. At the burnside turn right, ie. south-south-east, and on a thin grassy path travel with the burn for 250yds/m to join a 'shooter's' track, GR 356402, as it continues south-east to a burn junction. At this point, the nether regions of these steep-sided soft-topped hills, are surrounded by the scree slopes of Scawd Law and the heather of Priesthope Hill, with the only feasible exit being the course of Priesthope Burn.

A track winds south, through the silent valley, for ³/₄ mile/ 1.2km to the now sad ruin of Priesthope (3). Beyond, a gate opens into the coniferous jaws of Common Forest, below Back Craig, where the right fork in the forest road contours the south-eastern shoulder of Kirnie Law, by How Yards, for 1¹/₂ miles/2.4km. Curving around Purvis Hill ascend west to an intersection of incoming rides from Kirnie Law summit and Pirn Craig top. Turn left for a quick drop south-west on a grassy path via Pirn Craig to the pleasing broadleaves of Pirn Wood above Leithen Water and Innerleithen.

Accommodation, refreshments and services available in Innerleithen.

ITEMS OF INTEREST ALONG THE WAY

(1) INNERLEITHEN. Site of the burial place of a son of King Malcolm IV of Scotland, and of a 9th century sanctuary stone of close-grained white sandstone, known as the Runic Stone; its four faces decorated by cup-shaped hollows ringed by double circles. A mill town from the end of the 18th century, when the town's first woollen mill, Alexander Brodie's, was opened in 1790. Robert Burns, so the plaque states, visited on May 14th 1787, perhaps to take the famed spa waters at St Ronan's Wells, waters of high repute that were taken as a cure for ailments of a scorbutic, opthalmic or

dyspectic nature. The present day St Ronan's Interpretative Centre opens daily from Easter to October.

(2) THE RESERVOIR. Now a ruined enclosure, of football pitch dimensions, with walls 16ft/4.9m high, this reservoir was built for the mills of Walkerburn around 1920. Water was pumped up at night from the Tweed far below into the reservoir, in order to power the mills during the day. A pipeline led up via the pumping tower on the south-east flank of Kirnie Law. The system operated successfully until the 1939-1945 war. In 1990 the east wall was demolished with dynamite.

(3) PRIESTHOPE. A sad reminder of the decline of upland steadings in the Border hills. Such cottages, the Victorian replacement of the summer 'shieling' with a more substantial four seasons building, are now sightless and empty as the labour force of the out-by farm is reduced.

WALK 11: The Windlestraw Attraction

INNERLEITHEN - KIRNIE LAW - GLEDE KNOWE - WINDLESTRAW LAW - SCAWD LAW - CAIRN HILL - WALKERBURN - INNERLEITHEN

A varied and challenging walk that provides a viewing platform, of the Moorfoot Hills and beyond, that is second to none. This circular walk over ridge, summits and valley floor, of 12 miles/19.2km, ascends a total of 2323ft/708m, with a walking time of 6/6½ hours. Graded 3, the route treads forest paths, heathery tracks, peaty fells and grassy ways by riverbanks, making walking boots and hill-walking equipment a must. In poor visibility map-reading skills are essential.

ROUTE DIRECTIONS

Park at the free roadside car park in Leithen Road on the B709 overlooking Leithen Water. Walk north beyond the church, crossing Leithen Water on Cuddy Bridge, a narrow packhorse arch on the right. Once across turn right and then left, ascending the wooded spur of Pirn Wood, to a path rising north and north-east between crowded conifers before bursting out via open ground onto the remains of an Iron Age fort.

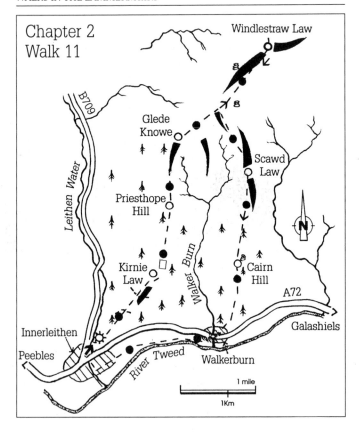

Chapter 2
Walk 11

Windlestraw Law

B709

Glede
Knowe

Scawd
Law

Leithen Water

Priesthope
Hill

Kirnie
Law

Walker Burn

Cairn
Hill

N

A72

Innerleithen

Peebles

Galashiels

River Tweed

Walkerburn

1 mile

1Km

Descend steeply, from the embankments and ditches on the
mound, by a lone telegraph pole, to enter the spruce once more on
a distinct path ascending north-east. As the rise continues to the top
of Pirn Craig (1), the trees open out revealing rock and scree on the
right and fine views beyond. A distinct twin-track then labours
north-north-east through more conifers for ³/₄ mile/1.2km to the
open heather-clad top of Kirnie Law (1). On breaking out of the
constricting conifers a fan of paths offer themselves for choice. Take
the more pronounced one that contours the hillside north-east, ie.

106

Windlestraw Law over Leithen Glen

right, and as the way swings left, ie. north, an old pumping station comes into view, with further surprises ahead. On the broad heather-clad col below there stands a bizarre concrete construction, The Reservoir (2), that defies description.

Beyond the giant rectangle continue north, on one of two heathery pathways, to the rounded top of Priesthope Hill, pausing awhile to gaze at the encircling panorama of writhing valleys and rolling hills, including the now extinct conical volcano of Lee Pen to the west. Once the flat top of Priesthope is attained a wall plus a wire fence are met; aids that will guide and support the walker over the switchback to the domes ahead. The descent, between fence and forest, to Priesthope Sware will no doubt be a hurried affair; the ascent of Corby Craigs and Glede Knowe most certainly with leisurely, or even laboured, steps.

For the final 2 miles / 3.2km north-east swing right to the summit, trig point and paraphernalia of Windlestraw Law (3), passing its twin top ³/₄ mile / 1.2km from Glede Knowe. The ascending path narrows and can be somewhat moist on this stretch, but with the fence always close navigation does not distract from the endless flow of visual delights.

Return south-west to the secondary top, noting the scattering of weathered rocks and two triangular cairns (4), one north of the fence and one on the south shoulder. Beyond the untidy stone pile on this secondary top an incoming fence from the south, ie. left, is joined; our navigator for the next $3^{1}/_{4}$ miles/5.2km. Here the distinct ridgeway allows the mind to soar and the legs to stretch, over Plover Knowe, Scawd Law and Cairn Hill, providing celestial views of upper Tweeddale.

From the cairned summit of Cairn Hill, with its breeze block ruin, descend south into the conifers on a grassy track passing a second cairn. At an angled bend leave the track, dropping steeply south on a narrow grassy trace running through the forest ride. As the roofs of Walkerburn become visible a wall is met which impedes further progress. Turn right with a distinct wallside path, first right and then to the farmhouse. Pass through the enclosed yard to emerge onto the A72 running through the centre of Walkerburn (5).

Cross the road walking south, then turn right at the school to pass the rugby ground, for a $2^{1}/_{4}$ mile/3.6km Tweedside stroll west to Innerleithen, which is entered via the caravan site en route to the main street and Leithen Road.

Accommodation and services in Innerleithen and Walkerburn.

ITEMS OF INTEREST ALONG THE WAY

(1) PIRN CRAIG & KIRNIE LAW. Exhibit classic examples of dykes, ie. intrusions of Old Red Sandstone injected from the earth's interior into cracks and fissures in the crust. These two hills also give clear indication of the direction of the Ice Age flow, from north-west to south-east, smoothing the western flanks and leaving the eastern leeward sides covered with boulder beds or scree (seen from the A72).

(2) THE RESERVOIR. A rectangular concrete reservoir, the size of a football pitch, built in 1919 as a prototype of the Cruachan Dam. The establishment of the National Grid in the Tweed valley marked the end of the reservoir.

(3) WINDLESTRAW LAW 2162ft/659m. Still spelt and pronounced locally as Windlestrae, the highest mountain in the Moorfoots

stands aloof from its fellow 2000-footers, separated by Leithen Water, Glentress Water, Dewar Burn and a glacial breach. Flat and dour on its upper reaches it nevertheless offers views of great magnitude and quality covering south-east Scotland. Within visual range to the north are the Lomond Hills of Fife, the Firth of Forth and the Pentland Hills, with the Manor Hills, Culter Hills and Broughton Heights filling the western horizons.

(4) TRIANGULAR CAIRNS. The two cairns, vertically and sectionally triangular on slabs of fell sandstone, are of a style unusual in the Borders. One is near to the summit fence and is alligned, at 210° magnetic, with a similar cairn on the same elevation some 150yds/m south of the secondary top of Windlestraw Law. Such erections apparently bear no relation to summits, boundaries, route markers or burial sites. Identical cairns are found on the Three Pikes ridge in North Tynedale, above Kielder Water reservoir.

(5) WALKERBURN. Its first woollen mill was opened in 1845 by Henry Ballantyne, a building that now houses the Scottish Museum of Textiles. A second 19th century listed building, of much interest and in good working order, stands by the south-east corner of our exit from the enclosed farmyard opening onto the A72: a Victorian cast-iron two-stall gents' urinal.

WALK 12: Highway to Peebles

INNERLEITHEN - LEE PEN - BLACK KNOWE - DUNSLAIR HEIGHTS - SHIELDGREEN - SOONHOPE BURN - PEEBLES

A linear walk, with regular bus connections between the start/finish, covering 11 high miles/17.6km that opens up this scenic corner of the Southern Uplands to all. The total height gain, on paths and tracks that provide easy passage, is 2316ft/706m achieved in a series of short sharp bursts in the first half of the adventure. Graded 3, it is recommended that walking boots/shoes and clothing for the conditions are worn; a map and compass in addition to providing peace of mind will also identify the surrounding tableaux of Border landscapes. An alternative route to Peebles, for the second half of the journey, descends through Glentress Forest, shortening the walk to 9¹/₂ miles/15.2km and reducing the ascents to 2152ft/656m. *The route description for this variation is listed under* **Walk 12A**.

ROUTE DIRECTIONS

From the crossroads at the west end of Innerleithen's main street walk north-west up Hall Street, bearing left at the end, with a tarmac road, making for the visible television mast on Caerlee Hill. North of the mast and the remains of a prehistoric fort, a path winds through heather and gorse rising to a stiled stone wall at the corner of a coniferous plantation. Looming ahead is the coned and beckoning bulk of Lee Pen, our first hurdle. Continue via the plantation wall over Kirklands Hill, through two metal gates, then finally on a zigzag path rising steeply through the boulder field to the spiky summit. Here a half-broken wall allows access to a broad twin track running north. As damage can be exacerbated by continuous use, it is suggested that the wall is crossed to the west side in the angle of the junction, where a few protruding stones and steps allow a careful crossing. Several summit outcrops please the eye and also provide fine seats from which to admire the surrounding upland scenery (1).

The wide heather-clad ridge stretching north and north-west, by fell and forest, over Lee Burn Head, Mill Rig, Black Knowe and Black Law, must surely tempt all of the outdoor persuasion as it flows into the distant skyline. On the west side of the guiding stone dyke/fence two thin paths trek through the heather, and at the first opportunity, ie. south of Lee Burn Head, cross to the east side at a break in the wall onto a grassy twin track that gobbles up the miles to Black Knowe and Black Law (2). At Black Knowe join the forest edge as the route ascends by Clog Knowe, topped by four pine poles (3), to the trig point of Black Law. This dark domed hill drops with some suddenness to Leithen Door, a narrow col allowing passage from the Tweed to Leithen Water, where a wicket rail leads to the south-west side of a crumbling dyke and fence. The breathless ascent north-west up Leithen Door Hill, between fence and forest, is assisted by a series of posts, no doubt to hang on to. ¹/₂ mile/0.8km beyond, a bridleway coming in from the open fell is met at a slip rail. At this point turn left into the tracked forest ride.

Follow this pathed ride as it winds above Horsburgh Hope, for

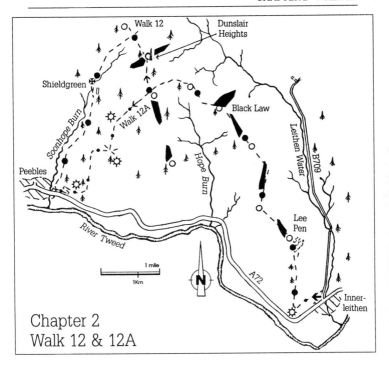

Chapter 2
Walk 12 & 12A

just over ¹/₂ mile/0.8km, to Caresman Hill, where, at the cross-tracks * - *AT THIS POINT THE ALTERNATIVE DESCENT TO PEEBLES, WALK 12A, BEGINS.*

Our way turns right with yet another old wall to Dunslair Heights, topped with a prominent tower bristling with antennae, the highest point on the walk. From here the remaining miles are descending ones, first north with the forest line on a peaty path to the col below Shieldgreen Kipps, then left with a grassy path (waymarked Cycle Way) that curves north-west on Tower Rig, high above a narrow glen and through the conifers for 1 mile/1.6km to Shieldgreen Tower (4) and Shieldgreen. Two forest roads are crossed to reach the site of Shieldgreen Tower, a sharp spur topped with an ageing rowan and a youthful larch growing through the moss-

Shieldgreen Tower - ruins and Shieldgreen Glen

covered masonry that was once a proud pele. Below the tower's
remains take the right fork, on the better track, to descend west and
south through a restructured stand to the rear of Shieldgreen
Outdoor Centre, Crookston Castle School, May 1975. The green-
shuttered house is passed around its north gable-end, where a left
turn brings the walker past the front to continue south and south-
west, with forest roads running parallel with Soonhope Burn,
eventually leaving the forest below Kittlegairy Hill. As a wooden
chalet village is passed the chimney pots of Peebles appear, beyond
the stables of the Hydro Hotel leading to the A72. Turn right, ie.
west, for the town centre (5).

WALK 12A: Highway Variations

AS WALK 12 FROM INNERLEITHEN TO CARESMAN HILL -
BLACK WAYMARKS TO GR 277411 BY CARDIE HILL - JANET'S
ROAD - PEEBLES

---

*AT THE CROSS TRACKS, a few yards north of Caresman Hill

summit, carry on west onto a wet forest track, a short feeder for a wide, waymarked black, forest road descending left, ie. south-west. Initially the way is 'a bit of a green tunnel' for 1 mile / 1.6km until it reaches a fork. Take the left-hand road and almost immediately a posted black and red waymark beckons from the forest fringe, indicating our path winds south-east and south, through a pleasing airy forest of venerable trees for ¹/₂ mile / 0.8km. Emerging above a large clearing and road junction where many incoming tracks and roads meet, a signpost 'To Peebles' directs us west-north-west onto Janet's Road forest track that loops above Linn Burn onto the forested Janet's Brae, liberally sprinkled with the remains of prehistoric forts (4), zigzagging onto the A72 at the east end of Peebles (5).

Accommodation and refreshments in Peebles or Innerleithen.

ITEMS OF INTEREST ALONG THE WAY

(1) LEE PEN. Derives its name from the pictish word *Pen* - end of, or head. Immediately east across Leithen Water glen the tops of Kirnie Law and Priesthope Hill lead north to the forbidding mass of Windlestraw Law with its supporting bastions of Bareback Knowe, Glentress Rig and Wallet Knowe, split assunder by Glentress Burn.

To the south-west and west the Manor Hills, the Culter Hills and Broughton Heights dominate the skyline above the silvery Tweed.

(2) BLACK LAW. Border hills are often named Black or White after the terms given to areas covered in heather (black lands), or matgrass (which turns white in autumn - white lands). As can be seen nomenclature given to both Law and Knowe is appropriate, for even the spruce skirt on the western slopes appears black.

(3) COMMUNICATIONS DEVICES? Two stout pine poles support a wooden frame bearing small mesh wire netting, some 6ft / 1.8km from the ground. There are two such erections, both facing the communications tower on Dunslair Heights. Such devices, albeit of a more sophisticated construction, can be seen on Mt Eacho, 3878ft / 1182m, above Elos in south-west Crete, where Nato radar devices sprout from many mountain tops.

(4) FORTS AND STRONGHOLDS. For centuries, even before the military engineers of Rome came to the Borders, the valleys of Lyne,

Eddleston and Tweed provided important, indeed the only, through routes to and from the Central Lowlands and the Borders. Therefore, considering the warlike nature of the local inhabitants and indeed the visitors, it is not surprising that forts, towers and peles, offensive or defensive, sprang up like mushrooms throughout the area. Favoured sites were spurs and shoulders, mainly around the 1000 to 1200ft/305 to 365m contour. Many examples can still be seen.

(4) PEEBLES. A bright and cheerful town, motto 'Peebles for Pleasure', was centuries ago the country retreat of many Scottish monarchs. From the past an old Mercat Cross and the ruins of Cross Kirk remain, together with many items in the Tweeddale Museum and Gallery; whilst present-day Peebles hosts annually an Arts Festival, Highland Games, Agricultural Show and the centuries-old Beltane Week.

WALK 13: The South Esk Horseshoe

GLADHOUSE RESERVOIR - SOUTH ESK - JEFFRIES CORSE - DUNDREICH - BOWBEAT HILL - EMLY BANK - BLACKHOPE SCAR - THE KIPPS - HIRENDEAN CASTLE - MOORFOOT - GLADHOUSE RESERVOIR

A high, wide and handsome tramp of 10^{1}/$_{2}$ miles/16.8km, over four rounded Corbetts and their flowing ridges. A journey, covering farm roads, grass tracks and paths that, at higher levels, also involves heather louping and peat hag bashing - fortunately accompanied by a guiding boundary fence. A height increase of 1778ft/542m is achieved if the horseshoe is completed in an anticlockwise direction, around the steep sided upper cirque and source of the river South Esk. A journey that rewards the tenacious walker with views north beyond compare. Graded 3, the horseshoe involves 5^{1}/$_{2}$ hours' walking time. Walking boots and gear for the conditions, plus map and compass, are recommended.

ROUTE DIRECTIONS

Access to parking, at the south end of the picturesque, but shallow, Gladhouse reservoir, is gained via a minor road running either east from the A703 at GR 245511 at Silverdean, or south from the B6372 at Upper Side. A signpost on the south side of this road at GR 285532

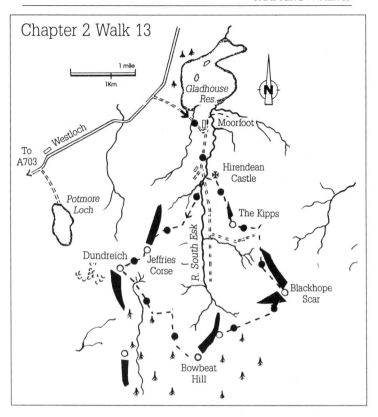

Chapter 2 Walk 13

1 mile
1Km

To A703

Westloch

Potmore Loch

Gladhouse Res.

Moorfoot

Hirendean Castle

The Kipps

Dundreich

Jeffries Corse

R. South Esk

Blackhope Scar

Bowbeat Hill

indicates Moorfoot; ³/₄ mile / 1.2km south-east provides parking on a grassy circle by the 'Gladhouse Reservoir' notice at GR 292528.

Walk south-east on the tarmacked lane for ¹/₂ mile / 0.4km to the farm of Moorfoot, a tempting start with Gladhouse reservoir behind and the leaping billows of the South Esk Horseshoe beckoning ahead. At the farm turn right, beyond the right-hand cottages, onto a farm road lined with a modern cattle court. This roadway, with two gates / cattle grids, is followed for approximately ¹/₂ mile / 0.4km south to Gladhouse Cottage, revealing the ruins of Hirendean Castle and The Kipps ahead. Prior to the cottage take the left fork, making for the sluice and fish-leap in the infant South Esk (1), where a narrow grass path on the right rises south-west with a feeder burn on the left.

Cross the burn, when a square sheep stell comes into view, onto a grassy path ascending the steep spur above, on a bearing of 200° magnetic, rising to a slip rail through the fence and onto the open fell. Once on the spur summit, with superb views north, the path descends west to the narrow col where a distinct twin-track is joined. Ascend with purpose, west and west-south-west, with the twin-track, faint in places, over grass and heather and finally peat for ³/₄ mile / 1.2km above Hawkster Gill Burn to a fence leading left to the flat, cairned summit of Jeffries Corse 2005ft / 611m.

The South Esk horseshoe, whilst presenting an apparent problem due to a cover of heather and naked peat cloaking the featureless hills, is safely negotiated and with some ease, thanks to a conveniently placed fence marking the boundary between Scottish Borders and Lothian. It provides 6 miles / 3.7km of guided walking from Jeffries Corse by descending south-west onto the bealach below Dundreich, ¹/₂ mile / 0.4km distant. A short diversion from the fence to the cairn and trig point on Dundreich 2041ft / 622m (2) is well worth the effort for it furnishes the walker with a panorama of scenic excellence. Return south-east over grass and heather to the guiding fence, close by the wet and marshy source of Leithen Water. Here a slip rail allows access onto a twin-track winding south and south-east through heather and marked with the odd guide post, well above the infant burn and boundary fence, to reach a finger of conifers probing east. Rejoin the fence as it swings east with the trees and at the apex leave them on a single path rising south and south-east for 1¹/₂ miles / 2.4km to the grass, heather and wild strawberry scattered summit of Bowbeat Hill 2051ft / 625m (3).

Continue north-east with the fence, via Emly Bank, to the damp and peaty bealach above Long Grain and the conifers of Craig Hope, for the mile-long haul north-east up Kings Road Nick and Long Edge to Blackhope Scar (on old maps Scaur) 2136ft / 651m. The highest point of the journey, its summit pock-marked with open wounds of weeping peat, it is a junction for three fences at the trig point and metal 'bird-table'.

Descend steadily north-west with the left-hand fence for

³/₄ mile / 1.2km, then swing right, ie. north, for a further ³/₄ mile / 1.2km, to an elbow in the fence leading north-north-east. At this point leave the fence left, ie. west, over open fell for the rounded top of The Kipps. A wide farm road drops sharply into the valley below - use only as an emergency escape route. Sixty feet / 18m below the top of The Kipps a twin-tracked path, slicing through the heather, is met. Veer left with the track contouring The Kipps. The track continues north, high above the valley, for ³/₄ mile / 1.2km to the shoulder of Hirendean Hill. Descend the steep spur, on a winding grass path, to the decaying mass of crumbling masonry that is Hirendean Castle (4), flanked by five venerable trees and a modern brick sheep stell - a fine place for mushrooms.

A cart track joins the South Esk, with its sluice and bridge, leading to Gladhouse Cottage and journey's end at Gladhouse reservoir.

Accommodation and refreshments at Eddleston or Leadburn.

ITEMS OF INTEREST ALONG THE WAY

(1) RIVER SOUTH ESK. Gurgles to life on the sombre northern flanks of Bowbeat Hill and Emly Bank, before it hurries through the narrow glen to swell the shallow reservoirs of Gladhouse and Rosebery (East of Scotland Water Authority joining the North Esk at Dalkeith and flowing into the sea at Musselburgh.

(2) DUNDREICH. Previously spelt Dundroich or Dundroidgh, the 'Mountain of the Druids' is reputed to have witnessed Druidical sacrifices many centuries ago. On certain days at certain times this heather and blood splashed fell can be a sombre moody place.

(3) BOWBEAT HILL. A watershed for the South Esk and Leithen Water, it is also known as Powbeat or Powbate, in which there is a spring so deep and mysterious as to suggest the mountain is one huge water vessel. This spawned the old rhyme of devastation should Bowbeat burst.

> *Powbate an ye breake*
> *Tak the Moorfoot in your gate,*
> *Huntly cot, a' three,*
> *Moorfoot and Maudslie*
> *Five kirks, and an abbacie.*

> Anon

(4) HIRENDEAN CASTLE. Now a leaning, teetering shell, sheltering sheep, vermin and stinging vegetation, this once proud 16th century pele stands sentinel no longer over the medieval grange and chapel of Moorfoot; a settlement within the protection of nearby Newbattle Abbey.

WALK 14: The Dundreich-Lee Pen Ridgeway

POTMORE LOCH - DUNDREICH - HOG KNOWES - CARDON LAW - MAKENESS & SHIELDGREEN KIPPS - DUNSLAIR HEIGHTS - BLACK LAW - LEE PEN - INNERLEITHEN

An invigorating and stimulating ridge walk of 14 linear miles/22.4km providing the walker with a varying and never-ending panorama of the Southern Uplands and the Border Hills. Involving a total height gain of 2893ft/882m, in a series of short sharp bursts, the route covers country lanes, farm tracks, forest roads and paths, thin peaty traces through heather and grass plus stretches of open fell. Graded 4, mainly for its length and steep sections, the journey repays the walker tenfold for the energy expended on this 7/8 hour experience, by providing exclusive and seldom-seen sights of the Borders and its upland wildlife. Walking boots/shoes and clothing to suit the conditions are as essential as water and emergency rations, map and compass, guidebook and camera, and the skills to utilise them all.

ROUTE DIRECTIONS

Access to the starting point is gained from the A703 road, 2³/₄ miles/ 4.4km south of Leadburn and 2¹/₂ miles/4km north from Eddleston, where a minor road winds east to the junction, GR 256515, with Potmore Loch, 200yds/m prior to Westloch Farm. Limited parking is available on the roadside verge, west of the gate.

From the T-junction walk south-south-east, on the hard core road, for ¹/₂ mile/0.8km to the tree-lined northern tip of Potmore Loch (1), a stretch totally dominated by Dundreich, whose bulky ridges lumber down to loch and glen. At the head of the loch (reservoir), with its stone valve, a notice directs us left over the small bridge and through a metal gate that requests us to 'Keep to the Track'. This grass and dirt gated track continues south-east and

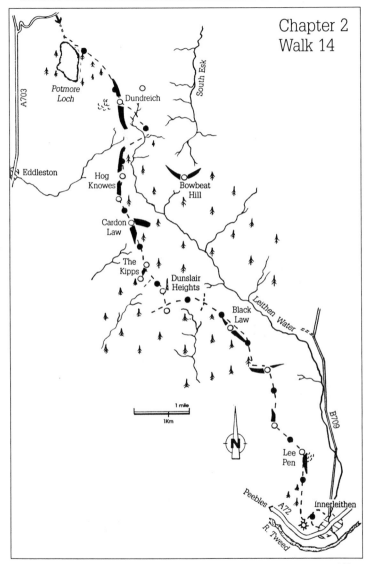

Chapter 2
Walk 14

south by the lochside and a stand of tall and proud Scots pine, to yet another gate.

Beyond the track forks, ascend left alongside the gloom of Fala Steel's close-planted conifers. A steady plod on a good track with the silent spruce leads to the apex. Here a stone dyke guides the pathway, deeply rutted in places, steeply south-south-east for approximately 1 mile/1.6km to the cairn and trig point of Dundreich (1).

Descend south-east from Dundreich, on a thin sheep trace, to join and cross, at a slip rail, a southbound fence by the wet and marshy source of Leithen Water. Ahead a vista of featureless hills, with a never-ending carpet of heather and weeping peat, presents an apparent problem which is in fact easily and safely negotiated due to the conveniently placed boundary fences of Scottish Borders and Forested Estates. Cross the fence and the rush-ridden Leithen Burn onto a twin-tracked path, with occasional marker posts, winding south high above the regional divide and Leithen Burn, to reach a finger of trees probing the ridge east.

As the conifers approach descend right, on a strip of white grass, to the junction of fell and forest by the confluence of Leithen Burn and a feeder burn. Cross the fence and burn to ascend west on a faint grassy path by the forest fence, meeting a distinct twin-track as the perimeter curves south with the ridge. Opening out onto an extensive panorama beyond Eddleston Water and Tweeddale, this point marks the beginning of a $2^{1/2}$ mile/4km undulating heathery ridge over the summits and cols, sometimes steep, of Hog Knowes, Howgate Nick, Longcote Hill, Cardon Law and the cones of Makeness and Shieldgreen Kipps (2). This is a breathtaking stretch with the tight forested glen of Leithen Water below to the east, scarred vertically by rushing water and home to roe deer, fox, buzzard and goshawk. On the col south of Cardon Law, with the distinctive rise of cairned Whiteside Edge to the west, a mire marks Witch Well, the source of Soonhope Burn - a well reputed to have been the one used to 'test' potential witches.

At Heathpool Forest, from Cardon Law to Shieldgreen Kipps, there have been recent private plantings of conifers on the western flanks. A wide ride with pathway runs south with the existing forest fence, and access has been approved, by the estate, for walkers

Lee Pen

along this route. This pathway must be adhered to at all times, thus respecting the owner's privacy and property; and as the area is extensively forested guard at all times against fire.

Leave Shieldgreen Kipps, via a narrow trace south, with wall and tree to the col below where a pathway, slithery with peat in places, ascends south to Dunslair Heights, communications tower *et al* (3), for a south-east glimpse of our final objective, Lee Pen. Continue south on the hard core road, only to leave via the footpath continuing south alongside a crumbling forest dyke, to a cross-track just prior to Caresman Hill. Take the pathway and ride left, ie. winding north-east and east, above Horsburgh Hope for ³/₄ mile/ 1.2km to the forest fence and open fell. At the slip rail our route turns right, ie. south-east, between forest and fence to mark the onset of the second half.

This high ridge is initially guided south-east by the forest march fence for 2 miles/3.2km; first a steep step down to Leithen Door, then a weary step up to Black Law and its trig point, passing Clog Knowe to reach an angled point in the forest fence just west of the domed summit of Black Knowe. The trees are left as Black Knowe is crossed. The route, still with fence and dyke, now surges south and south-east over Mill Rig and Lee Burn Head for 2 miles/3.2km, to the conical tip of that old volcano Lee Pen (4).

The east side, ie. left, of the wall provides an easier path but presents a problem on the summit, where an incoming wall has to be scaled; this is not advisable as the crumbling coping signifies. I would suggest the west-side path for the final stretch, with its rocky outcrops providing a delightful resting and viewing point.

Leave, no doubt with some regret, via the stone and scree clad southern slopes of Lee Pen, passing through two gates and by the conifers of Kirklands Hill to a stile, dropping to the prehistoric fort and present-day TV tower on Caerlee above the spa of St Ronan's Wells and the pleasing mill town of Innerleithen (5).

Accommodation and services available in Innerleithen.

ITEMS OF INTEREST ALONG THE WAY

(1) POTMORE LOCH & DUNDREICH HILL. Once famous for an abundance of eels, the loch provides a headstream of South Esk River which flows into the sea at Musselburgh. In the early 1800s there was an Earl of Potmore (the title is now extinct) and the lands formed part of the Black Barony estate - **Chapter 3, Walk 1**. Bishop Mackenzie, friend of the explorer David Livingstone, once lived in Potmore House.

Dundreich, its trig point at 2041ft/622m, its cairn at 2044ft/623m, known also as Dundroidgh, the 'Mountain of the Druids', is the most northerly of the high Moorfoots, commanding views of the Cheviots to the south and northwards, beyond the Pentlands, to the highlands of Perthshire. A sombre mountain that needs little from the imagination to conjure up the Druidical incantations and sacrifices over the blood-stained altar stones centuries ago.

(2) MAKENESS & SHIELDGREEN KIPPS. Occasionally the general mamillate form of the Border hills is broken by the appearance of peaky cones with very narrow summit ridges. Known as Kipps, they are the result of soft surfaces eroded away leaving harder, more durable but sharper peaks. These Kipps are seen to advantage from White Meldon - **Chapter 3, Walk 4**. Other examples are found in the Pentland Hills.

(3) DUNSLAIR HEIGHTS. Thought by some to be the jewel in the crown above Peebles, its top now bears a tall communications tower that is obviously more functional than decorative. Now clad and hidden beneath the Sitka spruce its title must, I feel, be claimed by The Kipps.

(4) LEE PEN. As its Celtic name implies - a sharp peak. Although not of 'Donald' height this conical ex-volcano is an outstanding landmark, a fitting example of mountain form to crown the southern end of a fine ridge. It also exhibits the classical leeward signs of naked rock and scree indicating the directional flow of the ice 10 million years ago.

(5) INNERLEITHEN & ST RONAN'S WELLS. On the skirt of Lee Pen surges a spring that was originally called Dow or Doo Well, a name derived from the well's attraction to flocks of local pigeons. In later years, when the curative powers of the waters had spread far and wide, and the Lord Traquair furnished the well with pump house, reading rooms and a veranda in 1826, the name of St Ronan's Wells was universal. The *habitués* of the spa began to take an interest in the St Ronan's Games and in 1827 forty-four noblemen and gentlemen banded together in competitions for prizes, and so the St Ronan's Border Games were born, games that still take place annually and include the celebration 'Cleikin' o' the Diel'.

CHAPTER 3
Cloich Hills and Broughton Heights

When our limbs are wearied and our spirit is done
We'll trudge to Cant's walls by the setting sun,
And then some hours we'll quaff a cup of ale,
And smoke our pipe, backed with a wanton tale.

Anon, Cant's Walls Inn

THE AREA

Two groups of winsome hills, though not high, wild or rugged are nevertheless aesthetically pleasing and can provide a stimulating challenge to mind and muscle. Whilst they lack a complementing loch or reservoir, and are in parts blanketed by regimented spruce, they nevertheless present an interestng canvas to those who enter into their secluded core. Clad by a picturesque patchwork of upland grasses and heathers in August and September, these highlight the braes and corries with a familiar white and purple sheen. Although semi-detached the two ranges display few similarities, that is apart from the binding crescent ridges. Indeed, due to the structure and form of the two groups, they are best seen when the shafts of the day's first and last light shadow and dapple their sinuous flanks. The south-eastern section of the area with its corrie-cleaved domed ridges, between Lyne and Broughton, has been designated a National Scenic Area by the Countryside Commission for Scotland.

The Cloich Hills have Flemington Burn as the principal water-course, rising from the ridges of Wether Law and Whaup Law, a lively burn that winds through steep sided fells to meet Lyne Water at Flemington. Hopehead Burn, its equivalent on Broughton Heights, springs to life between Pyked Stane and Wether Law - yet another Wether Law, emphasising the symbiotic relationship between hill and sheep - flowing leisurely south-east into Western Burn, prior to spilling into the Tweed at Stobo.

Both the Cloich Hills and the Broughton Heights were much

favoured by our prehistoric ancestors, as seen by the remains of hill forts and settlements peppering the spurs and the knowes. These circular camps, pre-dating the Romans, can be found on the Cloichs at Black Meldon, White Meldon, Drum Maw, Whiteside Hill, Harehope Hill and Hamildean Hill; and on the Broughton Heights at Muirburn Dreva, Kersknowe, Hoghill and Torbank. Our desire to walk the Border hills perhaps sprang from these ancestors, who carried water up to their settlements daily, for the majority of their settlements were at least 197ft/60m above the nearest spring. An example can be seen at Kersknowe where the spring is just above Easterknowe Farm.

The Cloich Hills, an ovoid group measuring $7^{1}/_{2}$ miles / 12km north to south and 5 miles / 8km east to west, has only seven tops rising above 1476ft/ 450m. Wether Law is the highest at 1571ft/479m, with Crailzie Hill, White Hope Shank, Peat Hill, Whauplaw Cairn, Stevenson Hill and Ewe Hill. There

Chapter 3 - Cloich Hills and Broughton Height

are however two domed hills of note and great popularity in the south, Black Meldon and White Meldon - 'the Hills of Fire' - whereas the Broughton Heights, a rhombic-shaped range of 6 miles/9.6km north/south and 7^{1}/$_4$ miles/11.6km east/west, sports nine tops above 1640ft/500m. Pyked Stane is, at 1873ft/571m, the highest, plus Green Law, Wether Law, Trahenna Hill, Brown Dod, Penvalla, Ladylurd Hill, Hammer Head and Broomy Side.

Both upland areas provide a combination of hill and valley walks, circular and linear, via rights of way, permissive paths or routes established over generations. A complete high-level circuit of all the tops is possible, though this requires careful planning in order to minimise repeated ascents. Their positions, roughly central on the Southern Upland rim, provide the walker with an encircling panorama and occasional glimpses of distant ranges. To the north, the Pentlands and the Firth of Forth, north-east, the Moorfoots, and south-east, the Tweedsmuir Hills haze the skyline. South-west, the immediate neighbours, the Culter Hills and the Biggar Gap, focus on the bulk of Tinto beyond the Clyde. It is said that, on a clear day, from the head of Stirkfield valley by Pyked Stane, the hills of the Isle of Arran can be seen, 75 miles/120km west.

Eddleston Water separates the Cloich Hills from the Moorfoots, and the waters of Tarth and Lyne restrain the Broughton Heights to the south-west. The Broughton Heights are divided from the Culter Hills by the Biggar Gap, through which Biggar Water ebbs and flows, and are bounded to the east by the Tweed and west by the flatlands of Back Burn and Candy Burn. Such waterways attract encircling main roads, allowing easy access.

The Cloich Hills are reached via the A703 Leadburn to Peebles, the A701 Edinburgh to Biggar, the B7059 from Romannobridge to the A72 by Drochil Castle, and the A72 Peebles to Biggar roads. An unclassified road from Eddleston to Lyne bisects the south-east corner into the Meldons.

Broughton Heights are also encircled by roads. Never penetrated, the A701 however clips the western corner to Broughton, while the A72 goes from Peebles to Biggar, the B712 from Lyne to the A701 south of Broughton, and the B7016 from Broughton to Biggar. The circle is completed to the west by the A72. A minor road, with no parking places, fringes the southern foothills from Broughton, via

Dreva, to the B712 at Dawyck.

Easy access to the hills is therefore ensured, though all approaches into their hearts must be on foot.

There are bus services from Edinburgh, Biggar and Peebles, and an early morning Post Bus. Timetables are available from bus stations and tourist information centres.

Habitation in the Cloich Hills and the Broughton Heights is spread thinly around the perimeter. Larger towns, Peebles for the Cloichs and Biggar for Broughton Heights, along with the villages of Eddleston, Leadburn, Romannobridge and Broughton, provide accommodation, services and supplies.

THE WALKS

Maps: OS 1:50,000 Landranger, Sheets 72, 73.
                   OS 1:25,000 Pathfinder, Sheets 459, 447, 448.
                   Harveys 1:40,000, The Walkers Map - Peebles.

CLOICH HILLS & MELDONS

Walk 1 circles west from Eddleston, via forest and fell, into the Cloich Hills. Walk 2, a linear atmospheric hike rich in wildlife, samples the wild isolated fells and forests from Romannobridge to Eddleston. Walk 3 treads an ancient circular way, alongside and above Lyne Water, over whistling fells and singing burns before returning to Romannobridge. Walk 4 treads the Hills of Fire, the Meldons both Black and White, for a varied walk with far reaching and revealing views.

BROUGHTON HEIGHTS

Walk 5, a pleasing linear walk, from Skirling to Broughton, of 3 miles / 4.8km provides tempting views into the range. Walk 6 enters and ascends the challenging tops and ridges of Hammer Head and Trahenna Hill. Not to be outdone Walk 7 goes just that little bit further beyond Pyked Stane on the Broughton Heights horseshoe, returning via two fine valleys. Walk 8 with a fresh approach, tackles solitary Penvalla from Tweedside and the parkland of Stobo. Walk 9 follows an old drove route from Broughton winding north and east through an upland valley and over two passes to the policies of Stobo. Finally Walk 10 provides the ultimate high-level circular traverse of the 13 tops of Broughton, a scenic and stimulating journey, worth every hard-won step!

INFORMATION TABLE

WALK	DISTANCE Miles/Kilometres		ASCENT Feet/Metre		D of D *	TIME Hours
1	10	16	928	283	3	5
2	8	12.8	801	244	2	4
3	7	11.2	735	224	2	3½
3 - Diversion	10	16	1325	404	3	5
4	3	4.8	1424	434	2½	2½
5	3	4.8	344	105	1	1¼
6	6¾	10.8	1391	424	3	3½
7	9¾	15.6	1772	540	3	5
8	8½	13.6	1463	446	3	4
9	6½	10.4	919	280	2	3
10	16	25.6	4006	1221	4	10

*Degree of Difficulty

1 - Good path, moderate ascent, no navigational problems.
2 - Distinct paths, steeper ascents, longer walk.
3 - Paths rough or indistinct, ascents demanding, navigation required.
4 - Walk long, demanding compass and mountain skills, high exposure.

Jeffries Corse (Ch.2. Walk 13)

Gladhouse reservoir and Hirendean Castle (Ch.2. Walk 13)

Hammer Head rig and Pyked Stane, from Grey Yade (Ch.3. Walk 6)

Stobo Kirk (Ch.3. Walk 9)

Broughton Heights

WALK 1: The Cloich Round

EDDLESTON - BLACK BARONY - FAIRYDEAN BURN - UPPER
STEWARTON - GREENSIDE/COURHOPE - KILRUBIE HILL -
WHAUP LAW - EWE HILL - UPPER STEWARTON - EDDLESTON

*A circular walk of 10 miles/16km, over fell and through forest, ascending
928ft/283m on cart tracks, grassy bridleways and forest roads. A route
offering tempting views of Eddleston Water valley and Moorfoot Hills
beyond, in addition to the Black and White Meldons and the distant Manor
Hills. Graded 3, this pleasing quiet walk can be completed in 5 hours.
Clothing to suit the conditions with walking boots/shoes recommended, as
is a flora & fauna guide.*

ROUTE DIRECTIONS
Eddleston (1), our starting point, straddles the busy A703 5 miles/
8km north of Peebles. Take care not to block access in Station Road
when parking. Start at the north end of the village, ascending on the
tarmac to Black Barony Hotel. At its wrought-iron gates our way
swings right onto a hard-core road that skirts the out-houses of the

hotel, crosses an 1859 bridge by Dean Cottage to wind by wire-meshed fence beyond Black Barony home farm and a pleasing copse of silver birch.

Once clear of the trees, turn left, ie. south, on a gated grassy track over Muir Plantation (an old toll road to and from Peebles), initially through heather, by guiding dykes/fences for 1 invigorating mile/1.6km, with mouth-watering views of the Moorfoots, the Manor and the Culter Hills to the east and south. After passing through a gate in the angled wall the old toll road is left, via a gate leading west, to the lone white cottage and roofless barn of Upper Stewarton (not named on the OS Landranger map). Beyond, the Sitka stands rise high on the Cloich Hills.

At the barn swing right between burn and fence as far as the wicket gate on the left (2); pass through and continue between wall and fence to the corner of the forest where a distinct but narrow path rises right, ie. west, through the trees. This pathway (shown on the

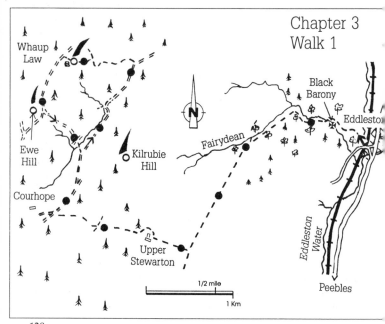

Chapter 3
Walk 1

Whaup Law

Black Barony

Eddlesto

Ewe Hill

Kilrubie Hill

Fairydean

Courhope

Eddleston Water

Upper Stewarton

1/2 mile
1 Km

Peebles

OS Landranger map), a waymarked right of way, passes initially through bracken and then on grass, zigzagging in places but overall west, for 1 mile / 1.6km, eventually emerging onto a wide hard-core forest road. A forest walk that is never claustrophobic and may reward the observant with sitings of grazing roe deer hinds and the lethal lines of a goshawk.

At the wide forest road turn right and continue ascending north-north-east, taking the left forks, above Courhope Burn for $^3/_4$ mile / 1.2km, between the tree-clad summits of Kilrubie Hill and Ewe Hill. As the way descends by an S-bend to the banks of the burn below Whaup Law (3), in the heart of the Cloich Hills (4), the deep treeless cleuch of Martyr's Dean tumbles down to a junction of rides and roads. Take the main forest road right, ie. north, as it ascends by an old quarry, for $^1/_2$ mile / 0.8km to cross Early Burn by the lay-by and wooden hide.

It is here that the energetic can gain reward for effort by ascending the wide ride west, with the larch. At what appears to be a dead end turn sharp right into a narrower ride, soon to meet an incoming ride from the left. Take this left turn for an ascending plod, on a narrow trace through tussock, west-south-west, before swinging west for the final yards to the cairned summit of Whaup Law (3). A pathed ride descends west from the cairn, soon to join a forest road. Turn left, ie. south-west, and south for $^1/_2$ mile / 0.8km to 40ft / 12m below the summit of Ewe Hill. On the eastern slopes of the summit turn sharp left, with a forest road, descending south-east for $^1/_2$ mile / 0.8km to pass a crossroads to Courhope Burn.

Once across the burn take the forest track right towards the buildings of Greenside / Courhope on our outward road; at the wide fork swing left and left again at the waymark. The way tracks east through the conifers to Upper Stewarton, returning to Black Barony and Eddleston.

Accommodation and refreshments available in Eddleston.

ITEMS OF INTEREST ALONG THE WAY.

(1) EDDLESTON. The existing church was rebuilt in 1829, to include masonry and the bronze bell of 1507 from the original church. 2 miles / 3.2km south is Redscaurhead, birthplace of George Kemp, architect of the Scott monument, who drowned before his Princes

Street masterpiece was completed.

(2) EAST of the WICKET GATE. A few yards from the gate the pasture is scored, with deep gouges and slightly raised embankments running north and south; markings that indicate either a Roman road, or a trade or drove route. The Roman theory can, I feel, be ruled out as the gouges/ditches and the flat land between have not the regular geometrical stamp of the Roman engineer. The uneven grooves, of a varied pattern, suggest strongly the regular passage of laden packhorses and/or driven cattle over the centuries; history relates a major drove and trade route ran from Cauldstane Slap in the Pentlands, through the Cloich Hills, to Peebles.

(3) WHAUP LAW. Ascribed to as Cloich Hill in 19th/20th century writings, and known locally as Whauplaw or Hill - *Whaup* being Lowland Scots for curlew. On the current OS Landranger map its untidy cairn is listed and named as Wauplaw Cairn 1519ft/463m.

(4) CLOICH. Listed in old charters as Auchencloich and Hardencloich, - Gaelic of the 10th to 12th century - *achadh*, a field.

WALK 2: Yesterday's Road - With Drover and Cadger
ROMANNOBRIDGE - DRUM MAW - FINGLAND BURN - GREENSIDE/COURHOPE-UPPER STEWARTON-FAIRYDEAN BURN - BLACK BARONY - EDDLESTON

An interesting drovers and cadgers route of 8 miles/12.8km through the Cloich Hills from Romannobridge on Lyne Water to Eddleston on Eddleston Water. The route is by cart track, grassy bridleways and forest paths, ascending 801ft/244m over windswept fell and sheltered forest, on waymarked paths through the spruce. An atmospheric hike, rich in wildlife - curlew on the fell, goshawk in the trees - offering a wealth of upland scenic delights. Wear clothing to suit the conditions overhead, with walking boots/shoes, on this grade 2 walk of approximately 4 hours.

ROUTE DIRECTIONS
Romannobridge (1), GR 161480, with parking and a pub, straddles the junction of B7059 and A701 by Lyne Water. From the junction walk north-east with the A701 for ¹/₂ mile/0.8km to Damside,

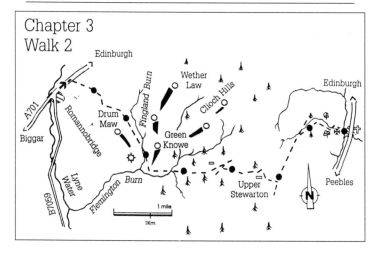

Chapter 3
Walk 2

Edinburgh

Wether Law

Clioch Hills

Edinburgh

A701

Biggar

Romannobridge

Drum Maw

Fingland Burn

Green Knowe

Lyne Water

B7059

Flemington Burn

Upper Stewarton

Peebles

N

1 mile

1Km

turning right at the cemetery, following the bridleway east past the farm of Romanno House on the right. An ascending and tree-lined angled track leads south-east over the open fell to the grass-clad bealach below the hump of Drum Maw, 1 mile/1.6km ahead.

Drum Maw is contoured via its north-eastern flanks, before descending into the green stillness of Fingland glen, tightly enclosed by Hag Law, Green Knowe, Drum Maw and White Knowe. The grassy, but rutted, track descending to the valley floor crosses the musical Fingland Burn before rising steadily up the grassy slopes of Green Knowe, to a junction of paths above the confluence of Fingland and Flemington Burns. A pleasing place to pause, as it offers views of interest (2), both at hand and on the hazy skyline. Swing left, ie. east, contouring the southern shoulder of Green Knowe, then leave the track by taking a narrow path right into the bracken, descending slightly, to a waymarked Forestry Commission gate above Flemington Burn. The waymark is a wooden post with white head and arrowhead, marked 'R of W'.

For the next ¹/₂ mile/0.8km the waymarked route winds east, ascending between Crailzie Hill and Ewe Hill, along silent and secretive alleyways of Sitka, carpeted with fading needles and wispy grass, eventually emerging by a steep-sided cleuch onto a wide forest road. Continue east with the winding way, passing the unplanted pastures surrounding Courhope, also named Greenside, Farm. Note the stepped ridge, to the north-west, leading to the cairned summit of Wether Law. Continue on the forest road bypassing the farm steading, and at the Y-junction of forest roads turn sharp right for 30yds/m to a waymark on the left, leading onto an east-bound track ascending through the trees.

This forest path continues east in a somewhat erratic fashion for 1 mile/1.6km, crossing a wide forest ride, before descending to the eastern extremity of the forest, where the north-eastern skyline, topped by the folds of mighty Dundreich **(Chapter 2, Walks 13 & 14)**, explodes into view. At the gated angle in the stone dyke ahead turn left, walking between dyke and fence for a short distance to a small wicket gate. Pass through, swinging right to the roofless barn and solitary white cottage of Upper Stewarton. Bear left, ie. east, with the cart track for 400yds/370m to a farm gate at the next wall junction. Immediately south the twin cones of the Black Meldon and White Meldon beckon invitingly; save them for Walk 4.

Turn left, through one gate to another leading onto a grassy bridleway north-north-east (a major drove road from Cauldstane Slap in the Pentlands to Peebles) with a guiding wall/fence on the right, for 1 mile/1.6km to the heathery and tree-clad banks of Fairydean Burn hurrying east to Black Barony (3). At the fork prior to the burn, swing right to the copse of silver birch and descend east on winding tree-lined ways, to the stables and coach house of the white turrets and towers of Black Barony Hotel, before journey's end at Eddleston and its church (4).

Accommodation and refreshments in Eddleston; for a wider selection Peebles lies 5 miles/8km south via the A703.

ITEMS OF INTEREST ALONG THE WAY

(1) ROMANNOBRIDGE. Named after the Romanno estate, not the occupying Romans. The original steep and narrow bridge of 1774, over Lyne Water by the old mill, provided the hamlet with much revenue, collected at the nearby Toll House of 1830, whose records of 1832 showed that in excess of half the income came from cattle droves. Iron-stone quarries in the 1800s and a poultry enterprise in the 1900s provided later revenue.

(2) OLD STEADINGS AND DYKES. West from Green Knowe, the south-east flank of Drum Maw is pock-marked with the remains of a prehistoric settlement and bisected with the grass-covered centuries-old stone dykes. Below to the south, on a burnside knowe, the lumpy pattern of a shieling's foundations can be seen, leading to the plateau of Stevenson Hill, beyond which the English lay in ambush, in the year 1304, for Wallace. On the distant skyline, the Manor Hills surround Manor valley.

(3) BLACK BARONY. From 1412 the seat of Murray of Haltoun, known as Black Barony. In the early 17th century the single tower was greatly strengthened and today's massive edifice resembles more a French chateau, with its lime tree avenue, than a Border stronghold. Black Barony is now a white hotel.

(5) EDDLESTON KIRK BELL. IC BEN OHEGOTEN INT JAR ONS HEERON MCCCCCVII. - "I was created in the year of our Lord 1507". A splendid bell of Flemish origin, it is thought to have been gifted by a Murray of Black Barony. It may also have rallied the men of Eddleston Water to that fateful field of Flodden in 1513, and to have tolled in sorrow later that October month.

Newlands Kirkyard - the Family grave

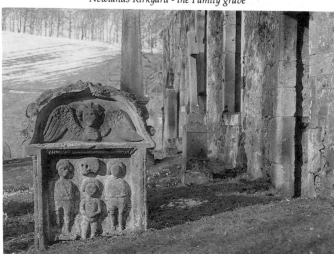

WALK 3: A Gypsies' Feud

ROMANNOBRIDGE - NEWLANDS CHURCH - WHITESIDE HILL - GREEN KNOWE - FINGLAND BURN - DRUM MAW - ROMANNOBRIDGE

Ancient cultivation terraces, a church thrown into confusion by Cromwell's approach, Iron Age hill-top forts, a drove road and a gipsies' battlefield can all be seen and studied on this scenic circuit of 7 miles/11.2km. Graded 2, the walk ascends 735ft/224m on distinct cart tracks and grassy paths. Should an ascent of Wether Law be included, the journey distance would be 10 miles/16km with a total height gain of 1325ft/404m, and be graded 3. The route over the ridge to Wether Law is not marked on the OS map as a footpath, although a grassy twin track is clearly visible and very practical; it would therefore be correct and courteous to seek permission before attempting this diversion. The route, providing solitude and far-ranging views, is never too taxing and can be completed in 3 ½ or 5 walking hours, but for full enjoyment take a little longer. Walking boots and clothes to match the conditions are needed, with a camera and map for memories and identification.

ROUTE DIRECTIONS

Romannobridge (1), astride the junction of the A701 Edinburgh to Broughton road, and the B6059, provides not only the beginning and the end of this walk but also parking (avoid blocking access).

Journey south, past the tiny Toll Cottage and dovecot road, with the B7059, for 1 mile / 1.6km passing Noblehall, into the picturesque jaws of the Lyne valley. Prior to the bridge across Lyne Water turn left beyond the 'new' Newlands church into the signposted lane, but not before treading the tree-lined old church path (2) south of the bridge. Our route then takes the lane climbing east and then south to the gated cottage of Whiteside, beyond which a grassy pathway passes through gates and dyke to contour south on the interesting slopes of Whiteside Hill (1) - 12th century terraces behind, 1st century BC fort above, and ahead the flat-floored valley of historic Lyne Water, with Drochil Castle (3) and the Broughton Heights.

As the track descends and zigzags east it merges, at a gateway, into a grass and dirt pathway above Flemington (4), to continue

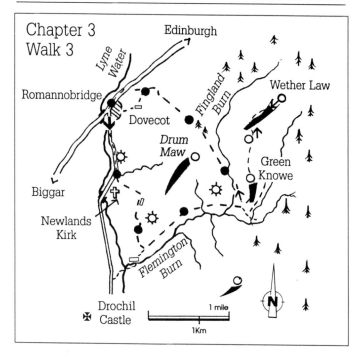

Chapter 3
Walk 3

Edinburgh

Romannobridge

Lyne Water

Dovecot

Finland Burn

Wether Law

Drum Maw

Green Knowe

Biggar

Newlands Kirk

Flemington Burn

Drochil Castle

1 mile

1Km

N

north-east above Flemington Burn. The path eventually joins a wider cart track that continues, above the loops of Flemington Burn, to an isolated collection of conifers, before swinging east for the rounded grassy shoulder of Green Knowe. A stimulating hike, silent but for the ever present calls of the moorland birds, with the skyline ahead dominated by the crinkly green ridge of Hag Law leading to Wether Law and the conifer-clad Cloich Hills.

At the confluence of Flemington and Fingland Burns below Green Knowe point, the gated way rises steeply to a junction of grassy tracks. It is from here that a diversion to the summit of Wether Law can be made by following the, initially steep, tracked way over the summit ridges of Green Knowe and Hag Law to the trig point of Wether Law, at 1572ft/479m the highest in the range. Return to Green Knowe point on the outward path.

From Green Knowe point descend north on the old drove way, to cross Fingland Burn, before rising north-west along the flanks of Drum Maw on a rutted cart track to a conifer stand (the OS map shows track and trees some distance apart - not so in fact). Pass through a gate into the trees and continue north-west, beyond a distraught quarry, for a gradual and pleasing oak and beech lined descent to the valley floor. At the footpathed A701 turn left at the cemetery for the last ¹/₂ mile/0.8km to the comforts of Romannobridge, with its dovecot (5).

Refreshments at Romannobridge.

ITEMS OF INTEREST ALONG THE WAY

(1) ROMANNOBRIDGE. A group of fourteen, well preserved, west-facing cultivation terraces can be seen just above the B7059 at Terrace Wood, south of Romannobridge at GR 162470. Thought to be the work of monks from Holyrood in the 12th century they were possibly linked with the terraces of Whiteside Hill GR 163457.

(2) NEWLANDS CHURCH. The original medieval kirk, with a restoration date of 1725, is now but ivy-clad debris, replaced in 1838 by the present church. In the original kirkyard is a selection of ancient tombstones, with perhaps the most interesting standing in the wall beside the manse bearing the fading lettering "Curis Viris". Cromwell strode by in 1650, causing the pulpit to issue the mobilisation of the Peeblesshire militia and to declare 'fast days' in an attempt to divert the approaching Roundheads. The now extinct Cant's Walls Inn (a verse extolling its virtues introduces Chapter 3) stood in the vicinity of Newlands kirk.

(3) DROCHIL CASTLE. Reports list its building in the 1580s for the Regent Morton, although it is said this Black Douglas never enjoyed occupancy due to a close encounter with the executioner's axe in 1581. Others state it was built in the 1560s for a "John Bold, indwaller (*inhabitant*) in the Towyr of Drochellis". Regardless of centuries past Drochil is today a sightless, roofless and windswept four-storey ruin.

(4) FLEMINGTON. In ageing accounts and on fading maps tabulated as Flemington Mill, a grain mill, one of many by Lyne Water held in high repute, as far back as the 1300s.

(5) GIPSY BLOOD. In October 1677 a longstanding feud erupted into a bloody battle between four gipsy families, the Faas (of Yetholm fame) and the Shaws against the Browns and Baillies. The feud festered throughout the recent Haddington Fair and ended in death; and as a result of the stramash at Romannobridge four Shaws were hanged in Edinburgh's Grassmarket in 1678. A nearby dovecot bore the anonymous couplet:

> 1683. *The field of gipsy blood, which here you see,*
> *A shelter to the harmless dove shall be.*

WALK 4: The Hills of Fire

MELDON BURN - WHITE MELDON - MELDON BURN - BLACK MELDON - MELDON BURN

The two conical 'Hills of Fire' are immensely popular with hill walkers and motorised picnicker's alike. A picturesque minor road, between Eddleston and Lyne, runs alongside Meldon Burn between the two hills, providing extensive parking areas and picnic sites at GR 212428. Solitude however still remains, above the 1000ft/305m contour line, on both steep-sided hills, and the visual rewards are well worth the ascent.

For a complete circuit of both summits, a more gratifying achievement, the statistics are - distance 3 miles/4.8km with a total height gain of 1424ft/ 434m. Graded 2¹/₂, both ascents need a walking time of 2 to 2¹/₂ hours. Should time allow only one Meldon, halve the figures given. The many crisscrossing dirt and grass paths and tracks, though steep, are well defined and in summer conditions well-soled trainers will suffice. In severe winter conditions hill-walking equipment is essential.

ROUTE DIRECTIONS

At the roadside at GR 212428, ¹/₄ mile / 400m south of the bealach, a public toilet, litter bins, information panels, picnic benches, and extensive car parking, below White Meldon and Black Meldon (1), mark the start of the walk. From the toilet block, by Harehope Burn, cross the road, stile and footbridge, ascending White Meldon east, via a narrow track through heather and bracken to the first of several 'steps or levels'. To the left on a flat spur is evidence of an Iron Age settlement or village (2). Continue climbing in a straight

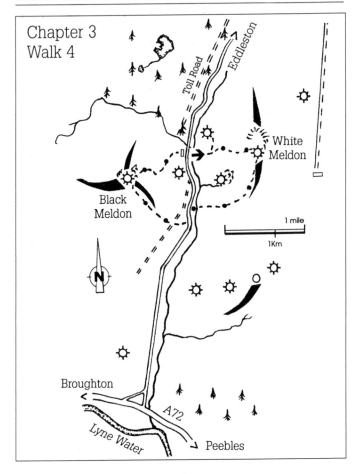

Chapter 3
Walk 4

Toll Road

Eddleston

White
Meldon

Black
Meldon

1 mile

1Km

N

Broughton

A72

Lyne Water

Peebles

line to reach an area of rocky outcrops which provide not only fine footholds but also welcome resting and viewing platforms high above the everyday sounds.

Winding east through the outcrops several grassy paths offer themselves to the walker, all leading to the summit, the choice simply determined by the ability and inclination of the individual.

140

Underfoot grass, rock and surrounding heather herald the summit, via three more 'levels'. White Meldon (3), capped with a large untidy cairn and a trig point perched on a rocky outcrop and ringed by the extensive embankments of an ancient fort, provides views beyond compare.

Descend the gentle southern shoulder for approximately $^1/_2$ mile/0.8km, swinging right, ie. south-west, before a boundary fence is met. The track leads to a slip rail in the fence. Do not pass through but continue to descend with the fence to the valley floor, where wooden cross-bars allow the fence to be crossed to a footbridge over the winding Meldon Burn.

In the car park west of the burn, by an information panel, a steep grassy path ascends north-west bisecting a cart track as it puffs its direct way over grass and heather to a distinct outcrop halfway to the summit of Black Meldon. Once the rocks are met pause awhile to drink in the glen and surrounding tops, before the final strides to the cairned fort topping Black Meldon. Another fine viewpoint, it gives perhaps even better views of Broughton Heights, Upper Tweeddale and Lyne Water. Descend from the summit, to the very visible starting point by Harehope Burn, via the rocky outcrops of ascent, then swing north-east onto a steep dirt and grass path flanked with bracken. This brings the walker directly to the starting point by the toilet block and car park.

Accommodation and refreshments available at Peebles.

ITEMS OF INTEREST ALONG THE WAY

(1) BLACK MELDON & WHITE MELDON. Meldon means 'The Hills of Fire', and both were places of worship for the Gadeni, an ancient Cymric tribe. As to the prefix of Black and White I would suggest they refer to the ground cover: a predominance of heather on the Black, and a predominance of matgrass (*Nardus stricta*), grass that bleaches white, on the White Meldon. Black and White are common prefixes for Border hills.

(2) SETTLEMENT. One of many such prehistoric (500 BC) settlements or defensive villages to be found in these hills. This circular stone-scattered settlement has three visible ditches and embankments to the east, the steep-sided west side having none. The enclosed centre provides evidence of 'horseshoe' dwellings, with the open end

facing south-east.

(3) WHITE MELDON SUMMIT & VIEWS. An extensive Iron Age and, later, Roman fort covered 9 acres of the high ground, the largest in Tweeddale, and is dated 300 BC. Surrounded by stone walls and ditches, it was found to contain burial cairns/cists, in which one cadaver was placed in each cist, in all probability a chieftain. The area today is littered with large stones, many grass covered and some in geometrical patterns.

As a Border viewing point White Meldon has few peers. To the north, beyond the flatlands of Hare Moss, is the saw-toothed line of the Pentland Hills; north-east the western rim of the Moorfoots topped by Dundreich and the three pointed cones of Makeness Kipps. South, beyond the curving Tweed, the heavy hills of Manor surround the U-shaped glen of Manor Water, whilst to the south-west Culter Fell glowers over the darkened folds of the Broughton Heights. White Meldon is an ideal place from which to plan future expeditions!

WALK 5: Introducing Broughton Heights

SKIRLING - WHINNYBRAE - SKIRLING CRAIGS - BURNETLAND HILL - CORSTANE HILL - BROUGHTON CHURCH & VILLAGE

An ideal sightseeing linear walk of 3 miles/4.8km (especially for backpackers approaching from the Biggar area), from which the form and pattern of the Broughton Heights eventually explode into view, whetting the appetite and pleasing the eye with sitings not available from the surrounding roads. The height gain of 344ft/105m is, apart from the initial ascent from Skirling, gradual for this grade 1 reconnoitre. Allow 1¼ hours' walking time, and as conditions underfoot do suffer from seasonal dampness wear walking boots/shoes. A map is also useful for identifying and planning future walks, in addition to studying the flatlands of Biggar Gap. One also cannot help but be immensely impressed by the giant Culter Hills to the south, no doubt with Chapter 4 in mind.

ROUTE DIRECTIONS
The white-washed strip of Skirling (1) straddles the A72, Biggar to Blyth Bridge, at GR 076391. Commence the walk at the tree-shaded
142

village green, leaving its north-eastern corner between a row of low cottages and a verandahed house, where a dirt and stone ascending track winds south-east to the tidy house of Whinnybrae. Beyond, at the conifers on the right, the cart track has a triple fork; take the centre way leading through a gate, or over a rickety stile, into a narrow strip of scrub and spruce ascending across the southern flanks of Skirling Craigs.

Little can be seen of distant views from this narrow enclosed path, although within, a rich selection of plant and bird life, including the plus of raspberries and the minus of prickly gorse. Once over the high point the way descends in a hurry to leave the trees, by the same method as entry, and cross Kirklawhill Burn to continue east on a metre-wide path, close to the guiding fence on the left. Double gates are passed at a field corner with a second fence on the left

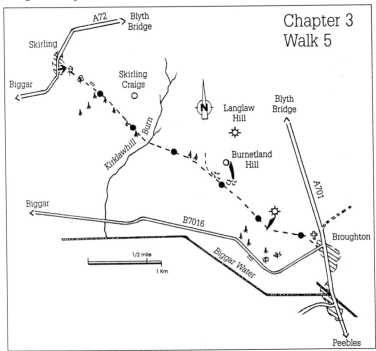

143

making for an under-nourished stand of pine below the domed cap of Burnetland Hill (2).

At the far corner of the trees yet another gate leads south-east on a distinct grass path, in places through rush infested wetlands, to the gorse-scattered southern flanks of Burnetland Hill, eventually to be channelled between two fences and a line of electric poles on an old stone-surfaced track. It is on this open section that great sights reveal themselves of Cardon Hill, and over the right shoulder the pencil-thin straight lines of Biggar Water lead the eye to the great rising deck of Tinto; with a promise of yet more to come as Burnetland Farm to the right is passed. The way now swings right, ie. beyond further gates, to run the gauntlet of encroaching gorse with rabbit-ridden burrows underfoot, before reaching the tree and gorse lined col of Corstane Hill.

Here the Broughton Heights are revealed, in all their shapely glory, filling the skyline to the north-east, as the wide way descends on grass-clad flanks to the tarmac by the kirkyard and ruins of Broughton Kirk (3). Only the north gable remains, crowned by a small bell tower and propped up by an earth-capped monk's cell. The lane continues into the pleasing and historic village of Broughton.

Accommodation and refreshments available.

ITEMS OF INTEREST ALONG THE WAY

(1) SKIRLING. It is recorded "that during a Presbyterial visitation in the 1600s the minister discoursed at length on St Matthew 10, verse 30; But the very hairs of your head are all numbered".

(2) BURNETLAND HILL. Assumed to have been named after the Norman family - de Barnveville or Burneville - who were granted land in the 1100s. A family who christened the first-born son Robert.

(3) BROUGHTON KIRK. On the site of a 12th century chapel, this is the small cell seen today. Also note the Haldane-Tweedie Memorial Tablet of 1725 in the kirkyard: two prominent families of these parts.

> *The Tweedies gart their noddles crack,*
> *like auld pot-metal, yank for yank.*

WALK 6: Hammer Head and Trahenna Appeal

BROUGHTON VILLAGE - BROUGHTON PLACE - HOLLOWS
BURN - HAMMER HEAD - TRAHENNA HILL - BROUGHTON
PLACE - BROUGHTON VILLAGE

*An invigorating circular journey onto the alluring, comely and scenically
revealing ridge connecting Hammer Head and Trahenna Hill, with a walk-
in via Hollows Burn that is instantly pleasing. This round trip of 6³/₄miles/
10.8km, with a direct height gain of 1391ft/424m, reveals breathtaking
views from the ridges and tops of Hammer Head and Trahenna. Underfoot
at lower levels are country lanes, grassy tracks and pathways; on the
heights and ridges, narrow traces through heather and rough grass.
Graded an easy 3, this delightful sightseeing round can be covered in 3¹/₂
interesting hours. Walking boots/shoes advisable, plus suitable clothing
for the time of year, on this walk that inspires the landscape photographer.*

ROUTE DIRECTIONS
Start from the village hall car park, GR 112368, at the north end of
Broughton (1), opposite the junction of the A701 and the B7016, to
Biggar.

Hurry along the first 200yds/m north on the busy A701, before
turning right into the peaceful safety of a tree-lined lane rising
gradually to Broughton Place Farm and Broughton Place, an
impressive mansion house of the 1930s now housing a gallery open
to the public. Call in on the return, for now the views ahead must be
exerting an unbearable pressure on the walker to explore the rising
ridges beyond the broadleaves and the shepherd's shieling to the
north. Here a springy grassy path aids the eager as it spears north-
east, passing plantations, long-gone gravel pits and bible-black
duck ponds, crossing and following Hollows Burn. One mile/
1.6km north of the ponds, as Hollows Burn is crossed at a wet and
boggy burnside area, leave the bridleway by turning acutely right,
ie. south, onto a twin track winding up the south-west shoulder of
Hammer Head (not the track into Green Lairs corrie). An ascent no
doubt stimulated by the inviting corries and gullies below the
crescent ridge to the right.

The ascending pathway snakes first south-south-east then north-
east up the grass and heather clad shoulder to join a fence labouring

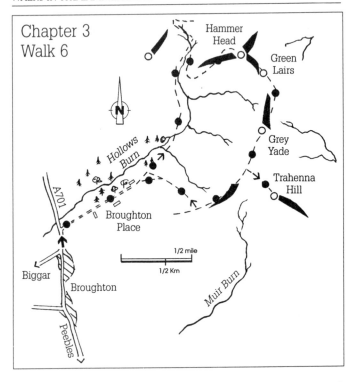

Chapter 3
Walk 6

Hammer Head

Green Lairs

Grey Yade

Trahenna Hill

Hollows Burn

A701

Broughton Place

Biggar

Broughton

Muir Burn

1/2 mile

1/2 Km

Peebles

east-north-east to the cairned summit of Hammer Head (2). Several small rocky outcrops pepper Hammer Head, the summit outcrop providing a convenient resting place from which to admire the surrounding countryside before striding along the curving ridge south-east, south and south-west with the guiding fence.

Stepping down with fence and half a dyke, on a distinct twin track through heather, the ridge rises and falls for 2 miles/3.2km over Green Lairs and Grey Yade to the fence junction leading to Trahenna Hill summit. A walk of character and scenic delights. Turn left, ie. south-east, on the saddle for Trahenna Hill, above a wide gully to the east and steep-sided Mere Cleuch to the south. Although somewhat moist underfoot alongside the fence, such hardships are only for $^{1}/_{2}$ mile / 0.8km. The grassy summit of Trahenna (3), with a solitary post and a pile of stones, is also a place to rest and contemplate the surrounds before returning to the main ridge.

Our way now descends, in a straight line south-west, on the westerly side of the dyke for $^{3}/_{4}$ mile / 1.2km to Cat Cleuch Head high above Broughton. As the dyke/fence angles right take the track away from the fence for a westerly descent through stubbly heather, over a spur, leading to a selection of grassy paths dipping down to Hollows Burn and the shepherd's shieling of our outward path. Before losing too much height cast a glance or two north over Earn Cleuch to the gracious folds of Hammer Head and Trahenna ridge, a memory to savour far beyond journey's end at Broughton.

Accommodation and refreshments at Broughton.

ITEMS OF INTEREST ALONG THE WAY

(1) BROUGHTON. Recorded first as Broctun - either a dwelling of Broc, or derived from *Brouch,* Anglo-Saxon for sheltered place. Broughton Burn, running through the present village, has its source high on the western flanks of Pyked Stane, the highest hill in the Broughton Heights and the point where the boundaries of Broughton, Stobo and Kirkurd parishes meet. Broughton today houses the John Buchan gallery, a local author who based many of his stirring tales in the nearby hills.

(2) HAMMER HEAD. The name arises from its wedge-shaped northern profile, and if confirmation be needed study the hill's contours on the map, which are aligned in the shape of a hammer head. With the range being so centrally placed on the rim of the Southern Uplands, Hammer Head provides one of the finest viewing platforms in southern Scotland, presenting a varied assortment, far and near, too numerous to mention but too good to ignore; take your map for a day of summit spotting.

(3) TRAHENNA HILL. The most southerly hill in the Heights and the southern bastion of the main ridge running north to Lochurd Hills. The slightly raised surfaces seen on the summit would suggest prehistoric occupation; if so, the tenants would also be privy to the superb views south and south-west of Tweeddale and Glenholm as they probe deep into the Tweedsmuir and Culter Hills. $1^{1}/_{2}$ miles /

147

2.4km south, above Biggar Water, lie the prominent remains of Dreva Craig Fort, Field Systems and Settlements; whilst a similar distance east, in the side of Dreva Wood, stands a quarry once famous for its roofing slates.

WALK 7: The Broughton Heights Horseshoe

BROUGHTON VILLAGE - BROUGHTON PLACE - CLOVER LAW PASS - GREEN HILL - PYKED STANE - BROWN DOD - HOPEHEAD BURN - HAMMER HEAD PASS - BROUGHTON VILLAGE

This horseshoe walk epitomises all that is good in hill walking, providing as it progresses immediate solitude, challenge without exhaustion or exposure, and high rewards in matters scenic, historical and natural. A journey of 9³/₄ miles/15.6km, involving ascents totalling 1772ft/540m, walking on country lanes, farm tracks, grassy paths and narrow dirt/peat paths through heather. Navigation even in poor visibility is fence/wall assisted by parish and forest boundaries for this grade 3 route, enabling the average walker to complete the walk in approximately 5 very pleasant hours. Walking boots plus appropriate clothing are needed, and on a clear day, with the aid of map and guidebook, the surrounding scenic highlights can be identified and appreciated.

ROUTE DIRECTIONS
The village of Broughton (1) stands on the junction of the A701 and the B7016, 5 miles/8km east of Biggar and 12¹/₂ miles/20km south-west from Peebles. Opposite the road junction, by the village hall, a spacious car park (free) marks the start of our walk, GR 112367.

Turn right, ie. north, onto the verge of the A701 for 200yds/m, then right again via a tarmac tree-lined lane rising north-east beyond Broughton Place Farm. At the baronial white walls of Broughton Place (2), continue north-east over a pillared cattle grid guarded by two mythical beasts with three-talloned fore feet, one smiling one snarling. A cart track lined with broadleaves makes a bee-line for the curves, cols and ridges of Hammer Head (**Walk 6**), encouraging a spritely step, past a shepherd's cottage, onto the open heather-clad fells. For the next 1¹/₂ miles/2.4km rise steadily north-

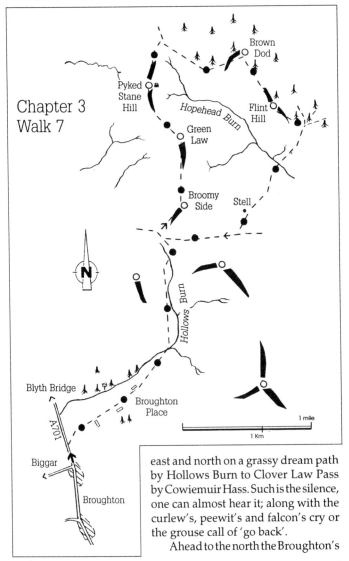

Chapter 3
Walk 7

Brown
Dod

Pyked
Stane
Hill

Hopehead Burn

Flint
Hill

Green
Law

Broomy
Side

Stell

N

Hollows Burn

Blyth Bridge

Broughton
Place

1 mile

1 Km

A701

Biggar

Broughton

east and north on a grassy dream path by Hollows Burn to Clover Law Pass by Cowiemuir Hass. Such is the silence, one can almost hear it; along with the curlew's, peewit's and falcon's cry or the grouse call of 'go back'.

Ahead to the north the Broughton's

ridge folds its grassy flanks over Broomy Side and Green Law to the summit of Pyked Stane and its top, Wether Law. A scenic walk, with its ups and downs, north-east and north with angled fence and dyke from Clover Law Pass, via grass paths and twin tracks on the east side of the fences. On the final few yards to the trig point of Pyked Stane, where three parish boundaries meet, should you be on the west side of the electric fence beware of the black water sink-hole.

At the flat top of Wether Law it's right wheel, with a squelchy twin track over peat, to the tree-fringed summit of Brown Dod. This is a fine vantage point from which to appreciate the horseshoe ridge encircling Hopehead corrie, with solitary Stobo Hopehead Farm nestling in its centre. Once over Brown Dod the pathway rejoins the forest fence sloping south to the rippling ridge of Flint Hill, providing tantalising glimpses of the Pentland Hills to the north. The heathery descent to Flint Hill col, onto the bridleway from Ladyurd, is steep; it is advisable to plot progress across the rush-clad enclosed basin of Hopehead valley before descending from Flint Hill.

Turn right at the col, passing south through bracken and winding down to the rush-ridden surrounds of Hopehead Burn, helped along by a fence-line. Once the burn is crossed swing right, ie. south-west, with the pathway and fence rising to higher, drier ground, where the fence/old wall are left. From this point utilise the thin sheep tracks, with two sheep stells (4) and Clover Law beyond acting as markers. Fractionally above the stells a wide grassy track can be seen rising steadily to Hammer Head Pass.

At the head of the pass turn onto our outward path for a scenic return to Broughton. A route enriched with the classically dignified outlines of Cardon Hill, Chapelgill Hill and Culter Hill gracing the southerly skyline.

Accommodation and refreshments at Broughton and nearby Biggar.

ITEMS OF INTEREST ALONG THE WAY

(1) BROUGHTON. In 1617 James VI passed through "Broughtoun and Tuedail" on his journey to England. The Privy Council ordered that on the day of 17th July fifty horses be provided by the county, "in reddyness at Broughtoun for his Majesteis carriage and household stuff".

Green Law and Pyked Stane summit ridge

(2) BROUGHTON PLACE. Despite its defensive centuries-old appearance, this towered house was designed by Sir Basil Spence and completed in 1937. A similar design can be seen at Kilbucho Place a mile or so west of Broughton. The original Broughton House, sadly gutted by fire, was owned in the 1700s by the infamous traitor Murray, and it was later sold to James Dickson, a Kelso entrepreneur whose fortune was greatly enhanced by Albermarle's sacking of Havana.

(3) PYKED STANE, 1872ft/571m. *Pyked* - coming to a point, *stane* - stone, though not named, only listed as 571m on the OS Landranger map, but thankfully named on the Pathfinder map 459, and referred to on older maps as Pyket Stave, *stave* - the curved piece of a cask. Distant vistas of all points of the compass can be enjoyed, including Arran, the Perthshire Highlands, Tinto's isolated bulk and the Tweedsmuir giants beyond Tweed.

(4) SHEEP STELLS. These stone-built sheep shelters are found in every upland Border glen, but not of such a shape or quality as the two above Well Burn. All are round, square or rectangular, except this unique Hopehead pair which are symmetrically hexagonal; ideally suited to protect against gusting winter winds. I would welcome reports on such shelters.

WALK 8: The Penvalla Loop

STOBO CHURCH - HARROWHOPE - HAMMER KNOWE - MID
HILL - PENVALLA - LADYURD HILL - HARROW BURN -
EASTON BURN - STOBO CHURCH

A 'tennis-racquet' hill walk, where the relatively short walk-in and walk-out is covered by the 'grip' with the circular 'frame' representing the greater part of the journey. A scenically varied walk of 8¹/₂ miles/13.6km, from pastoral tree-lined Tweedside to the windswept fells that rise in the prehistoric heart of the Broughton Heights. The ascent totals 1463ft/446m to the domed steep-sided cone of Penvalla and the flat summit ridge of Ladyurd; where from both tops the surrounding upland scenery presents a pleasing picture. For part of the journey it uses a way much favoured by drover and moss-trooper. Graded an easy 3, the route calls for stout footwear and hill clothing in addition to basic map-reading skills in order to achieve maximum enjoyment from this 4 hour walk.

ROUTE DIRECTIONS
Stobo (1) GR 184376 is a small and ancient Tweeddale hamlet of few houses lining the B712, running north-east with the strengthening Tweed some 6 miles/9.6km south-west from Peebles. Parking by Stobo Kirk (2) (please avoid service times) and Stobo Beekeeping Centre.

From the telephone box at Stobo turn left onto a dirt and stone vehicle track, signposted Easterknowe Farm, heading north-west past tidy cottages and Easton Burn. At the last cottage with its footbridge, and the road to Easterknowe on the right, pass through a metal field gate on a cart track following and crossing the course of Easton Burn west for 1¹/₂ miles/2.4km to the ruined steading and house of Harrowhope. It is a gradual ascent that for much of its way is lined with a fine mix of broadleaves and conifers, and pastured soft rising hills carrying the forts of centuries past (3); a way that eventually reveals the cone of Penvalla through a stand of venerable Scots pine. At Harrowhope swing left, crossing Harrow Burn by ford or rickety footbridge, to take the right fork ascending north-west between a finger of larch and Scots pine, via a gate, onto and over the heath of Hammer Rig for approximately 1 mile/1.6km to a fork branching right, ie. north. This fine open track passes by a sad

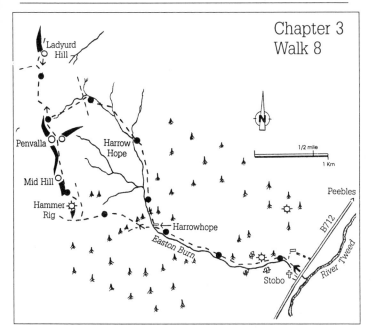

Chapter 3
Walk 8

and sparse pine plantation where, close by the site of an old homestead, a grass twin track twists sharp left to ascend north, above Hammer Knowe with its fort and settlement (3), up the heathery east flank of Mid Hill and higher still, Penvalla.

Initially a steep ascent of 330ft / 100m for the first ¹/₂ mile / 0.8km, the pulse rate confirming the tight contour lines, but thereafter a steady stepped way to the flat and lonely twin tops of Penvalla. Its name, as does nearby Penveny, suggests a Cumbric tribal connection (4). As with all the Broughton Heights the views from Penvalla are far reaching and awe-inspiring, and it is with some reluctance that Penvalla's very steep northern slopes are tackled to the col below.

From here a narrow path between crumbling wall and wire fence rises north to the long narrow top of Ladyurd Hill, the middle of the three pimples, which is the summit. Yet another grandstand from which to enjoy the views north, in particular the Pentland Hills. Return south on the path of ascent to the col between Penvalla

153

and Ladyurd Hill. At the slip rail swing left, to leave the old wall, onto a grass track descending the gully east with the infant Harrow Burn to the floor of Harrow Hope.

A pathway travelling south-south-east is met, and as it forks take the left branch to gradually descend with the true left bank of Harrow Burn leading to the proud Scots pine by the ruins of Harrowhope. A pleasing, if somewhat damp, route that reveals the great bulk of Penvalla's dished eastern flank and Huskie Rig. At Harrowhope turn onto our outward path for a reverse view of the trees and waters of Easton Burn leading to Stobo.

Accommodation and refreshments at Broughton or Peebles.

ITEMS OF INTEREST ALONG THE WAY

(1) STOBO. The name of the hamlet and parish of Stobo has had eighteen different spellings over the ages, eg. Stoboc 1116, Stobhope 1208, Stobhowe - the Hollow of the Stumps, and finally Stobo in 1473. The parish boundary abuts those of Broughton and Kirkurd on the summit of Pyked Stane, to the west of Stobo village.

(2) STOBO CHURCH. This restored medieval kirk, with its vaulted ceiling, housed for many years the local school - that is until a parliamentary decree in 1633 declared "a school building in every parish". So it came to pass that around 1640 Stobo had a new and separate school, but sadly for the parish no provision was made for the dominie. Not until 1745 did the local landowners agree to pay a legal salary to the schoolmaster, whose predecessors had survived by indulging in a spot of ecclesiastical or fiscal moonlighting. The payment of a full and legal salary prompted the cryptic entry into the kirk's records, "No Mortifications in Stobo".

(3) PREHISTORIC PRESENCE. The remains of forts, settlements and tumuli can be found on the knowes and spurs of Kerr's Knowe above Easterhouse Farm, Hammer Knowe, Huskie Knowe and Harrow Hope. Dated late BC / early AD, thus pre-dating the Romans of whom extensive evidence can be found at nearby Lyne, the settlements and forts consist of outer ramparts encircling thick walls. Secondary occupation, if any, is indicated within by the presence of horseshoe ring houses. As the wet, ill-drained valley floors were unsuitable and indefensible, all save one of these 'camps' were built between the contours of 951ft/290m and 1247ft/

380m. However, not all was perfection, for at Kerr's Knowe fort the nearest source of drinking water was 260ft/80m below, necessitating a repetitive and tedious ascent when full pitchers of water were required.

(4) BRITISH/PICTISH tribes, who created systems of 'Celtic' fields and Iron Age fortified hill-top settlements, have had their place names adopted by Anglian speakers. In this case, Northumbrians, who conquered them politically but coexisted peacefully. *Penn/pen* - end or head.

WALK 9: Broughton to Stobo - The Packhorse Trail

BROUGHTON - HOLLOWS BURN - HAMMER HEAD PASS - HOPEHEAD RIG - HAMMER RIG - HARROWHOPE - EASTON BURN - STOBO

A linear walk of 6¹/₂ miles/10.4km from Broughton to Stobo through the picturesque heart of the Broughton Heights; a mini-version of the popular West Highland Way, as it weaves through steep-sided valleys flanked by shapely hills. A gradual height gain, totalling 919ft/280m, will never break the stride, whilst still providing that heart of the hills feeling. The route covers old trade and drove ways (1), marked as paths and cart tracks on the OS maps, over distinct grassy paths and dirt twin tracks, beginning and ending at two villages of character and antiquity. This 3 hour, grade 2 ramble can be enjoyed wearing stout trainers/lightweight boots and clothing for the climate, not forgetting camera and binoculars to record the abundance of scenery and wildlife along the way.

ROUTE DIRECTIONS

By starting at Broughton on the A701, 5 miles/8km east of Biggar and 12¹/₂ miles/20km south-west from Peebles, the walker has the breeze on the back and the sun over the shoulder, thus harnessing the elements to advantage. From the village hall car park, GR 112368, hurry north for 200yds/m on the verge of the busy A701 before turning right onto the tree-flanked lane leading north-east to the water-wheel at Broughton Place Farm and baronial tower house of Broughton Place.

Once the gauntlet of cattle grid and mythical beasts has been run

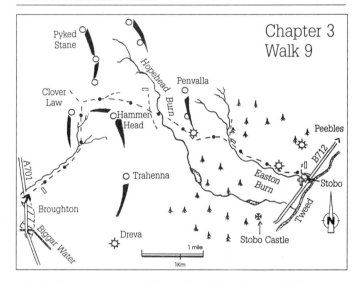

and the large presence of Broughton Place inspected the route opens out beyond the gated shepherd's cottage to the beckoning hills beyond. For the next mile / 1.6km north an inviting grassy track winds by Duck Pond Plantation, complete with pond, and Hollows Burn through Broughton Hope to Hammer Head Pass. A walk that lightens the step and swivels the head, as new vistas are revealed, for the corried crescent ridge of Trahenna and Hammer Head to the east, ie. right, landscaped with heather bracken and white grass, is a compelling and compulsive sight. The pathway divide of Hammer Head Pass is met below Broomy Side just beyond a network of feeder burns; take the right-hand track descending east to a fenced slip rail lying low between the slopes of Hammer Head and Broomy Side.

For 2 miles / 3.2km the heathery and variable path, in places thin and not too distinct, treks east and south (Penvalla's summit is a good marker) through this Shangri La of solitude into the hub of the Heights, passing the source of Well Burn, crossing Hopehead Rig with its twin six-sided stells, over Margate Burn and Hopehead Burn below the mass of Penvalla and Mid Hill before the cart track running alongside Hammer Knowe to the pass with Hammer Rig.

Harrowhope and Penvalla

The route is a haven for wildlife (2), impressively and completely encircled by the eleven tops above. From Hammer Rig descend between larch and Scots pine to the sightless stones of roofless Harrowhope where Harrow Burn, hurrying in from the north changes, as if by magic, into Easton Burn.

From this point our winding way with Easton Burn to Stobo is metamorphosed from isolated open fell to a tree-lined pastoral route, alive with birdsong, overlooked by the remains of Iron Age forts above. Stately ash, oak and beech blend well with the occasional dark green plantations and a single redwood points to Penvalla above the parklands of Stobo Castle. Stobo (3), with its fine old historical kirk and its beekeeping centre, is reached via a metal gate and a lane of pleasing burnside cottages.

Accommodation, refreshments at Broughton, Biggar and Tweedsmuir.

ITEMS OF INTEREST ALONG THE WAY

(1) DROVE & TRADE ROADS. Armstrong's map of 1775 states "There is a road called Stobo" which referred to the trade and drove

road from Lyne, and points north, connecting with the Thief's Road over the Manor Hills. Well above the undrained valley floors these 'Ways or Rodes' crisscross the higher, drier ground of the Southern Uplands and Border Hills, and conveyed clerics and cadgers, military might and those they pursued, plus many thousands of black highland cattle that trundled annually, legally or illegally, through these upland areas.

Three such feeder routes servicing the main thoroughfares ran through the Broughton Heights, betwixt Skirling, Broughton and Stobo, Broughton and Ladyurd, plus Stobo to Lyne Water by Hamildean.

(2) WILDLIFE. A route rich in moorland birds, the air alive with the distinctive cries of curlew (whaup), plover (peewit), snipe and grouse. Whilst herons, ring ouzels (mountain blackbirds) frequent the burns, the observant may catch a glimpse of a hen harrier skimming the heather.

(3) STOBO. A parish of character, that centuries ago was happy to welcome parishioners from its neighbouring parishes. In the nearby parish of Lyne in the mid 1600s, ploughman James Hay of Scrogs was summoned to appear before the kirk sessions to answer the charge of "playing football and dancing on the Sabbath". He admitted playing football, but said it was his wife who danced, and that in future they would attend Stobo Kirk.

Stobo Kirk contains many weathered headstones dating back to the late 1600s. They grace both yard and wall, where one may refer to James Hay and his dancing wife. Also on the wall at the kirk's arched entrance hangs a chained and padlocked 'Jougs', the old Scottish pillory of chained and padlocked iron neck-ring, from the French *joug* - a yoke.

WALK 10: Bagging Thirteen Broughtons

BROUGHTON - TRAHENNA HILL - GREY YADE - GREEN LAIRS - HAMMER HEAD - PENVALLA - LADYURD HILL - BROWN DOD - LOCHURD HILLS - WETHER LAW - PYKED STANE - GREEN LAW - BROOMY SIDE - CLOVER LAW - BROUGHTON

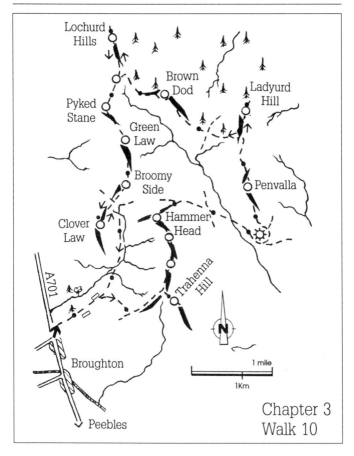

A circular high-level route that assaults all thirteen Broughton tops above 1600ft/488m, an up and down adventure, scenically rewarding and challengingly varied for experienced and fit hill walkers. Although no single top in the range exceeds 1872ft/571m in height, the circuit accumulates a total height gain of 4006ft/1221m over a total distance of 16 miles/25.6km. Underfoot, cart tracks, twin tracks, grassy paths and on the open fells and tops, thin dirt paths through heather and in places peat;

159

always visible, and along the high ridges guided by stone dyke and wire fence. Wet patches are more likely to be encountered than naked rock on this grade 4 walk of approximately 10 hours. Walking gear and equipment to suit the conditions overhead and underfoot are essential, together with map, compass, guidebook and adequate supplies of water and high-energy snacks. Three low-level points en route provide practical escape ways.

The anticlockwise approach to the circuit is less of a strain on legs and lungs, as it allows descent, not ascent on the extremely steep sections of Penvalla and Hammer Head. Also, the start at Broughton at 6am permits the anticlockwise route to reach the highest point, Pyked Stane, at 12pm, when energy levels are still high; leaving a descending ridge, with no sharp ascents, and a gradual downward sloping valley for the return half of the journey.

ROUTE DIRECTIONS

Broughton, a small ribbon of a village, straddles the junction of the A701 and the B7016; 5 miles/8km east of Biggar and 12$^{1/2}$ miles/ 20km west-south-west from Peebles. A village car park (free) adjoins the village hall GR 112368, east of the A701, opposite the incoming B7016 from Biggar.

Dash north on the pathless A701 for 200yds, adopting a more leisurely pace as you turn right onto a leafy lane rising north-east to Broughton Place Farm and the mansion house of Broughton Place - see **Walks 6 &7**. Beyond, the pastoral surrounds soon give way to the open fells, as the avenue of trees diminishes at the solitary cottage; the ascents begin here.

The glen ahead and its grassy track may beckon but our way soon leaves this 'fiddler's green' for higher paths, by turning right just beyond the cottage gate, where a distinct path rises east over the heathery flanks of Cat Cleuch Head. Continue with the twin track for 1$^{1/4}$ miles/2km to join a wall/fence ascending north-east, in a kindly way, for a further $^{3/4}$ mile/1.2km to our first top, Trahenna Hill. Its grassy summit rises, a short distance east from the wall junction beyond the damp watershed, offering views of upper Tweeddale fringed by the hills of Tweedsmuir and Culter.

Return west to the wall junction to begin a northerly traverse of the inviting crescent ridge covering the tops of Grey Yade and Green Lairs to Hammer Head - see **Walk 6**. With fence, small wall and twin track to guide the step, mind and thoughts can concentrate

Harrow Burn to Harrowhope (ruined farmhouse) (Ch.3. Walk 9)

Culter Hills from Hollows Glen (Ch.3. Walk 10)

Culter Waterhead and Culter Hills to the south (Ch.4. Walk 3)

Sunset over Yearngill Head (Ch.4. Walk 7)

Broughton Heights north over Hopehead Burn

on the day's journey and the unfolding sights that continuously delight the eye. From the small posted cairn on Hammer Head leave the ridge, no doubt reluctantly, by crossing the fence and low wall to descend north-north-east for 540yds / 500m, via a broad shoulder, on an initially zigzagging twin track by a line of rotting fence posts, to Hopehead Rig. There join a narrow pathway, through heather, traversing right, ie. east, across the basin of Hopehead - see **Walk 9**.

So pleasing is this basin crossing, with surrounding heights and ever present wildlife for company, that it must surely be 'All things to Some walkers or at least Some things to All walkers' as it winds east and south-east, crossing Margate and Hopehead Burns to rise with a track ascending the flanks of Hammer Knowe to Hammer Rig Pass (an escape route to Stobo). East of the pass branch left with the track heading north, encircling the Iron Age fort on Hammer Knowe, to swing left onto a grassy twin track beyond a bunch of ailing and ageing pines. This convenient track winds steeply north through the heathery eastern slopes of Mid Hill, topped with a sad wee cairn, to the twin tops of noble Penvalla, high above Pear Burn corrie - see **Walk 8**. A summit rewarding the anticlockwise walker, for who would wish to ascend those severe northern slopes?

From between the twin tops of Penvalla a faint path north promptly delivers the walker onto the domed col below, from where a thin path, sandwiched between fence and wall, angles up to the narrow extended summit ridge of Ladyurd Hill. From its centre summit the pyramid of North Berwick Law, fringing the Firth of Forth, can be seen, as can the entire range of the Pentland Hills leading to Scotland's capital. Ladyurd is a strong candidate, along with Brown Dod, as a summertime stop for refreshments; perhaps a little exposed to the thin north-easters in winter. Return from the centre top, for a short distance, to the forest fence junction, turn right and follow the tree boundary descending west to the col and its bisecting path below Flint Hill (an escape route to Ladyurd).

The heather is strong and deep, the path thin and the slope steep, as the rolling ridge of Flint Hill is ascended alongside the forest fence before an easier passage tops the domed pate of Brown Dod. Continue, down and up, with the conifers to Lochurd Hills, a way that allows tantalising glimpses of distant vistas through natural and man-made gaps in the spruce. From Lochurd Hills walk south on the summit ridge, over terrain that favours webbed feet, to the scarcely discernible top of Wether Law, which leads by fence to the obvious trig-pointed summit of Pyked Stane, the highest point of our circuit - see **Walk 7**. This grandstand allows all acts of nature's show to be enjoyed with ease and wonder, in particular big Tinto to the south-west and beyond on the hazy horizon Goat Fell on the Isle of Arran.

Keeping to the east side of the guiding fence, the well-named Green Law and then Broomy Side soon slip by as the ridge splits at Clover Law Pass (an escape point for Broughton). Having come this far the steady ¹/₂ mile/0.8km ascent, south-south-west with the guiding wall to Clover Law the last top, will present no problems. The reward from this somewhat flat top is the views south of the Biggar gap and Glenholm probing into the stately profiles of the Culter Hills (**Chapter 4**). The high life is left by returning to Clover Law Pass, turning right and descending south with grassy path and tinkling Hollows Burn; a burn that changes its name to The Dean as it runs through the wooded glen prior to joining Broughton Burn, for the final delightful 1¹/₂ miles/2.4km to Broughton Place and finally Broughton village.

Welcome accommodation, refreshments at Broughton, Biggar and Tweedsmuir.

CHAPTER 4
The Culter Hills

How wild and harsh the moorland music floats,
When clamerous Curlew scream with long drawn notes;
And here the lonely lapwing whoops along,
That piercing shrieks her still-repeated song.

John Leyden

THE AREA

Culter, pronounced 'Cooter', is the spelling for the Hills, the Fell, the Water and some Farms. Coulter, an old spelling, is used for the Village and most Farms, originally meaning the fore-iron of a plough share somewhat similar to the profile of Culter Fell. A series of riven ridges and rounded tops that rise south of the Broughton Heights provides a staunch western bastion for the upper Tweed as it tumbles north from its source at Tweeds Well, before swinging north-east at Drumelzier. This point marks the eastern end of that flat phenomenon, the Biggar Gap, through which flowed the River Clyde when the earth was young. These seldom walked feral fells of Culter proudly supply a link in the northern rim of the Southern Uplands, and in doing so provide two national watersheds: one from Wills Cleuch Head to Scawdmans Hill for Tweed and Clyde and onwards to the North Sea and the Irish Sea; the other, by Beattock Summit, between the rivers of Annan and Clyde, sheds water to the Firths of Solway and Clyde. Many deep cleuchs scar and score the steep hillsides west of the main north-south ridge, a constant reminder, as are the four reservoirs, of hurrying water. No such indicators exist on the drier eastern flanks of the Culter Fell Ridge, where water-washed naked shale and reservoirs cannot be found.

Several prominent glens and their associated burns, becks, gills and grains radiate from the main central ridge, rather like spokes in a wheel in which the judicious placement of dams has created the four reservoirs of Culter Waterhead, Camps Water, Midlock Water

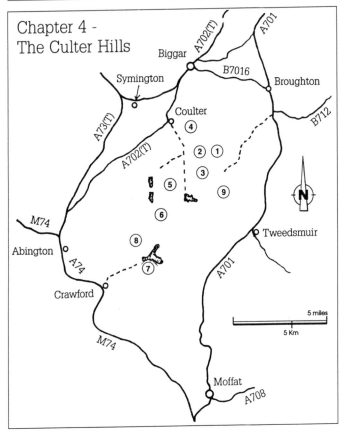

Chapter 4 -
The Culter Hills

and Wandel Water. All flow west into the Clyde, with the dam of Camps Water Reservoir forming the largest reservoir of the four. Both Culter Water and Cow Gill, which feeds into Culter Water then the Clyde, run north through narrow steep-sided glens that contain reservoirs; not so the eastern glens of Kingledoors Burn (house spelt Kingledores), Holms Water and Kilbucho Burn. All three feed the Tweed from the central and eastern Culter Hills and tend to be drier than their western brethren, with the extensive horizontal floor of

Kilbucho glen providing additional geological and historical interest. A glacial breach created a floor so flat that excess water ebbs and flows both east and west below the small rounded hills that are peppered with prehistoric forts and settlements, and where once stood a crannog (fortified island).

Ringing this ovoid area, some 10 miles/16km wide and 15 miles/24km long, a collection of roads and rivers allows easy access to the perimeter from all directions. The B7016 covers the northern marches, running through the Biggar Gap from Biggar to Broughton where it links with the A701 on the eastern fringes, and the A702 on the bounds of the western side. The A701 from Peebles to Moffat runs alongside the River Tweed, servicing traffic from Edinburgh, the Borders and Carlisle, whilst the A702 close by the River Clyde connects with the A73(T) from Strathclyde and the A74(T) from the M6 and Lockerbie. As with the majority of Border hill ranges, minor roads and tracks can only tentatively probe the interior, though with little success, for no vehicular way emerges at the other side. Entry to the Culter's central ridge is gained by using the following minor roads/tracks: 1 mile/1.6km south from Broughton and east of Culter Fell, south-west via Holms Water to Glenkirk; south from Coulter village to Culter Waterhead Reservoir or south-west to the two reservoirs of Cowgill; and finally east from Crawford on a minor road alongside Camps Water to Camps reservoir.

A range, with few inhabitants and even fewer settlements, in the black and white mould of rolling and ridged Border hills, the Culter range appears as an upland plateau rent assunder by the ravages of some primeval axe-man, so steep and savage are the open wounds of cleuch and gully that score and scar the rounded domes of hill and ridge. Five summits and three tops exceed 2000ft/610m, and all cluster, in a loose U, in the north-eastern quadrant overlooking a collection of spidery reservoirs that supply Strathclyde. By following the lead of the gaffer - Culter Fell 2454ft/748m and its top Moss Law 1886ft/575m - the walker is offered a selection of adventurous mountain and ridge routes above Culter Waterhead reservoir and the lonely glens of Glenholm and Kingledoor.

The ubiquitous conifer has made a stand, particularly on the lower southern and south-western slopes, but fortunately not in enough numbers to change the character of these secluded uplands.

These uplands remain predominantly heather and grass covered, a characteristic that could present navigational problems in adverse weather or poor visibility due mainly to the close proximity of clustered look-alikes, with few pathways, no waymarks or signposts. This potential problem is eased and assisted by the many county and parish boundary fences/stone dykes running along the ridges and over the summits. An example is Scottish Borders boundary fence, running roughly north to south for $14^{1/2}$ miles/23.2km over or close to the maim summits and their connecting ridges, conveniently providing a guiding hand. Such aids allow the walker to appreciate the surrounding hills, without having to refer constantly to guidebook and/or map.

Accommodation and refreshments can be obtained at hotels, inns, guesthouses and bed and breakfasts in Moffat, Crawford, Abington, Biggar, Peebles and in the majority of small villages scattered along the surrounding roads. A few farmhouse B&Bs are available on the fringes of the range, with a youth hostel at Wanlockhead and camping at Wiston Lodge.

Public transport - bus services: Edinburgh to Coulter, Crawford daily, and Moffat Friday to Sunday; Biggar to Broughton, Peebles to Broughton, Monday to Saturday. A postbus at present runs from Biggar to Tweedsmuir, Monday to Saturday.

THE WALKS

Maps: OS Landranger 1:50,000, Sheet 72.
                     OS Pathfinder 1:25,000, Sheets 459, 471.

Walk 1 stalks the three big ones around the East Face of Culter, whilst Walk 2, Culter Fell Direct, also ascends Culter Fell by a route that is easier than first impressions indicate and opens up this compact range for all to see. Walk 3, By Ridge and Reservoir, also ascends the highest mountain in the range, this time by a more varied route. Walk 4, Forts, Terraces and Crannog, in complete contrast skirts the foothills in search of the past. The Hudderstone Loop gives Walk 5 a buzzard's-eye view of this split and scarred range above the reservoirs of Cowgill and Culter Waterhead; as does Walk 6, The Windgate Gap & Kyegill Slop, a hill walk that stimulates and rewards the enthusiast. Walk 7 circumnavigates the silvery waters of Camps Reservoir. Walk 8, The Diel's Barn Door, looks down upon Duncan Gill from Whitelaw Brae and the mysterious cleuch. Walk 9 is a scenic linear traverse through the northern half of the range from Coulter village to Holms Water.

INFORMATION TABLE				
WALK	**DISTANCE** Miles/Kilometres		**ASCENT** Feet/Metres		**D of D** *	**TIME** Hours
1	9½	15.2	2149	655	4	5½
2	8½	13.6	1640	500	3	4½
3	7	11.2	1634	498	4	4
4	4½	7.2	541	165	2	3
5	7½	12	1493	455	3	4
6	9	14.4	1526	465	3	5
7	5½	8.8	131	40	1	2½
8	9	14.4	1302	397	3	4½
9	11¾	18.8	2152	656	4	6

*Degree of Difficulty
1 - Good path, moderate ascent, no navigational problems.
2 - Distinct paths, steeper ascents, longer walk.
3 - Paths rough or indistinct, ascents demanding, navigation required.
4 - Walk long, demanding compass and mountain skills, high exposure.

Culter Hills

WALK 1: The East Face of Culter Fell

GLENKIRK - HOLMS WATERHEAD - LEISHFOOT HILL -
CULTER FELL - KING BANK HEAD - CARDON HILL - BIRNIES
BOWROCK - CHAPELGILL HILL - CONGRIE RIG - GLENHARVIE
BURN - GLENKIRK

*A circular hill walk of 9¹/₂ miles/15.2km, encompassing the two highest
Donalds, Culter Fell and Chapelgill Hill and the highest top, Cardon Hill,
in the range. Although the mountains are steep and bare they display a
dignity of outline, with smooth sweeps to their summits, that makes them
an irresistible challenge for the walker. Approached from Holms Water
glen (also known as Glenholm), the total height gain on the circuit is
2149ft/655m. It is mainly on fell tracks and pathways over grass and
heather, which may in places be wet and peaty, however such minor
irritants immediately vanish as far flung vistas unfold. Although relatively
short this ascent of Culter Fell, the highest in the range, and its two
outlyers, is in no way a 'tourist route'. The grading of 4 is due mainly to
the unrelenting steep ascents and high exposure above Culter Fell's east
face. Mountain boots and correct outdoor equipment for the conditions are*

as essential as map, compass, camera and binoculars; and be prepared to encounter more wildlife than fellow walkers on this aerial adventure of 5¹/₂ hours.

ROUTE DIRECTIONS

Calzeat (1), south of Broughton on the A701, stands at the entrance to Glenholm, a valley that is entered via a signposted minor road

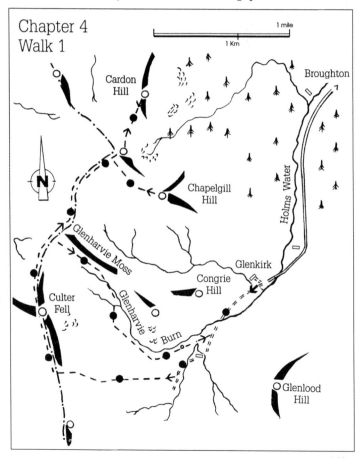

Chapelgill and Cardon Hills from Culter Fell

running south-west and south from the A701 at GR 115342. This narrow road runs with Holms Water for 4 miles/6.4km to the buttressed heights of Chapelgill, Cardon Hills and Culter Fell, before crossing Holms Water by the lonely steading of Glenkirk (2), the start/finish of our walk. Limited parking on roadside or wallside verges, though do take care not to block access and also ensure that your presence does not disturb the farming cycle, particularly during lambing (April).

From Glenkirk follow the dirt road south-west to the cottage of Holms Waterhead - no doubt accompanied by the whaup's plaintive cry - passing Congrie Hill and Glenharvie Craig to reveal the steep, corried east face of Culter Fell. Also seen is our guiding fence, rising from beyond Holms Waterhead west through white grass and heather, on the broad shoulder of Leishfoot Hill to the south ridge of Culter Fell towering above. A fence, reached by slip rail/gate from the new dirt road, ascends steeply west for 1¼ miles/2km to the fence junction at the summit ridge. Spare a moment during ascent to cast your eye right, over Glenharvie Rig, above Glenharvie Burn running south-east from Glenharvie Moss. Over the rig and alongside the burn a twin track runs down to meet Holms Water by a sheep stell; your path of return from the high ridges.

Turn right, climbing north on a good pathway over a series of annoying false tops, to reach the raised trig point of Culter Fell 2454ft/748m, a viewing platform that is breathtaking, in particular the immediate views, south-east over Culter Waterhead reservoir and north-north-east over the cleuchs of Glenharvie and Hope to the sweeping rigs and domes of Chapelgill and Cardon. When fully satiated continue north, descending steeply with the fence as it curves through the saddle of bible-black hags on King Bank Head. To experienced Chevioteers they will present no problems; for those who have not had the happy experiences of The Cheviot the thin paths on either side of the fence spearing north allow safe passage.

A steady incline leads via Dun Knees to a junction of many fences marked by an untidy pile of slabbed Felsite topped by a metal pole. It is here the boundary fence turns sharp north-west, and it is here at Birnies Bowrock, often mistaken in poor visibility for Cardon, that we continue north for ½ mile/0.8km to the flat distinctive peak of Cardon Hill 2215ft/675m (3). Look west beyond North Hope Burn to the abrupt darkness of Scawdmans Hill, north for the winsome sweep of Broughton Heights, and south-east over the severe cleuch of Cardon Burn to the drawn-out summit of Chapelgill Hill 2283ft/696m.

Return to Birnies Bowrock and approximately 90yds/m beyond the wee cairn leave the fence on a distinct path winding and rising south-east through heather, grass and peat to the flat and barely distinguishable top of Chapelgill. Ridge and top provide grand close-ups of Culter's east face, and mountain hares bouncing over the heather. After a revealing scenic wander on the grassy summit return via the outward path north-west to the fence. Swing left with the fence over the hags on King Bank Head to a slip rail in the fence. This 'rail' marks a narrowing, tracked ridge leading south-east to Glenharvie Craig between the burns of Hope and Glenharvie.

Continue for approximately ½ mile/0.8km on the ridge to its narrowest point and descend south, ie. right, on the now distinct winding track to join Glenharvie Burn as it gains in strength, below the east face of Culter, to hurry down to the sheep stell by Holms

Water. The curlews will still be circling to pipe you back to Glenkirk.
Accommodation and refreshments at Broughton.

ITEMS OF INTEREST ALONG THE WAY

(1) CALZEAT - pronounced Callate. An old inn stood by the parish church at the yett of Holms Water, bearing the inviting sign 'Call late or Call sune, Y'ell get drink 'till your money's dune'. So inviting was the inn that on cold stormy nights the kirk congregation of seven, plus the minister, adjourned to the inn, refreshments being ordered "for the good of the house".

(2) GLENKIRK. Home for centuries to the family of Porteous, a scion of which resided at Hawkshaw near Falla Moss, and it was his men who captured sixteen of Cromwell's men returning to Biggar. A Porteous ordered "fell them one by one with a mall (mallet) and fling them in Falla Moss". One escaped but threw himself off the cliff at Glencraig. In the 1800s local 'herds dug fifteen Ironsides out of Falla Moss.

(3) FROM CARDON HILL. $2^{1/2}$ miles / 4km north-north-west from the summit, over White Hill on the north side of Kilbucho glen, lies Crosscryne. It was here, when it was known as Corscryne, that the English camped, in 1207, before the battle of Biggar; a battle not recognized by conventional historians as the tale rests mainly in the 'verse' of Blind Harry. Corscryne also marked the English-Scots boundary in 1334.

WALK 2: Culter Fell Direct

BIRTHWOOD - FELL SHIN - CULTER FELL - MOSS LAW - HOLM NICK - CULTER WATERHEAD RESERVOIR - CULTER WATER - BIRTHWOOD

The shortest distance between two points is a straight line, and our route, Culter Fell Direct, ascends over the heather of Shin Fell direct to the grassy summit of Culter Fell of that Ilk. A prominent and dominant summit standing at 2454ft/748m. The price for this direct assault to Culter Fell's trig point is the height gain of 1640ft/500m in $1^{3/4}$ miles/2.8km; the value, a fine array of views and future walks, both near and far, from this top of *the range summit. Thereafter our way is downhill, save for an unnoticeable 66ft/20m incline to Moss Law, for this journey totalling 8½ miles/13.6km. Graded 3, it provides a fine ascent, airy ridge walking, a reservoir stroll and a pleasing valley walk over grassy tracks and paths, dirt roads and a country lane. Wear walking boots and hill clothing, particularly in adverse weather, and carry map, compass and camera.*

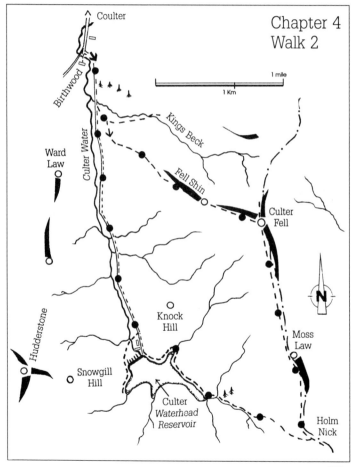

Chapter 4
Walk 2

ROUTE DIRECTIONS

Close by the mansion of Birthwood, GR 031311, 2 miles/3.2km south from Coulter village, there is limited parking just beyond the sign 'No unauthorised vehicles', on the grass and hard-core verge by Culter Water. Follow the tarmacked, beech-lined road and burn south for ¹/₂ mile/0.8km to the confluence of Kings Beck and Culter Water (1) where, beyond the bridge, a cart track climbs left towards the rearing bulk of Fell Shin.

This track rises steadily south-east and at the first fork swing right onto a grassy twin track leading steeply skywards to a line of vintage, stone shooting butts linked by a distinct peat and stone path. These butts indicate that the surrounding heather bears annual witness to the hatching and dispatching of grouse, therefore please keep to the paths, without your dog, during nesting and avoid the area during the shooting season. Beyond the butts and the first skyline the path continues ever upwards on its south-east course. Indeed for the next mile the grass/peaty track is always obvious, even under winter's snow when it bears evidence of sheep and fox. Aided occasionally by post or cairn, it ascends over a series of giant steps to the rather flat and grassy apex of Culter Fell (2), complete with trig point and north-south fence.

Descend south for 1 mile/1.6km on the broad ridge, guided by a wire fence, to the grassy pimple that is Moss Law. A slight diversion west from the pathway reveals the spidery reservoir of Culter Waterhead shimmering below the scarred flanks of Snowgill Hill, Hudderstone, and Dod Hill. South from Moss Law the fence and path drop 361ft/110m in ¹/₂ mile/0.8km to the watershed of Holm Nick; water trickling north via Holms Water reaches the North Sea, the flow west via Culter Water ending in the Irish Sea.

At Holm Nick a wide and stony road eases west-north-west with Culter Water, jinking through sloping fell shoulders past a stand of sad conifers, a five-bar gate and sheep pens to reach the eastern extremity of Culter Waterhead reservoir (3). Along its north shore continue to the dam and houses at Culter Waterhead. The final 2¹/₂ miles/4km north are alongside the bows of Culter Water, where the narrow road with wide verges runs beneath the dark and dominant domes of Knock Hill - **Walk 3**, Woodycleuch Dod and Ward Law - **Walk 5**, before reaching the venerable beeches of

Birthwood.

Accommodation and refreshments in Biggar.

ITEMS OF INTEREST ALONG THE WAY

(1) STREAMS & BURNS. The many rushing tinkling streams and burns in this range are referred to by a mixture of names - burn, beck, gill, grain and houp, indicating different races with varied tongues have passed this way, for beck and gill are more common in the Yorkshire Dales and the English Lake District than in the Border country.

(2) CULTER FELL. Offers far-reaching views on a clear day: north to the Perthshire Highlands - Ben Vorlich and Ben More, south to the serrated northern profile of the English Lake District, and west to the Firth of Clyde with the Isle of Arran.

(3) CULTER WATERHEAD RESERVOIR. To date, the property of Strathclyde Water Services, as are all the reservoirs in the Culter Hills. An authority that allows genuine walkers and lovers of the countryside access to the reservoir areas; but please observe the instructional notices.

Conceived in 1900 to supply Motherwell and Wishaw, it was not until 9 January 1908 that the valves were closed and the reservoir filled, only to spring a leak in the bank which was repaired the following summer by pumping in liquid cement. The many delays were due initially to road and rail, standard and narrow gauge, construction; later however the main cause was the transportation of Puddle Clay, especially in winter conditions. In February 1906 "over 50 wagons loaded with clay were on the ground or at the railway siding, and there appears no hope of getting them emptied".

During construction, by Robert McAlpine & Sons of Glasgow, a temporary village was built at Culter Waterhead, consisting of navvies' huts, grocer's store, school, mission house and canteen. Traces of the rail tracks, probably narrow gauge, are still discernible by the stone-built measuring house and the trestle bridge over the spillway.

Walk 3: By Reservoir & Ridge

BIRTHWOOD - CULTER WATERHEAD - BREEKS BURN & LANG GILL - CULTER FELL - KINGS BECK CORRIE - KINGS BECK - BIRTHWOOD

A varied and challenging walk, not long but packed with interest for every step of the circular 7 miles/11.2km. By country lanes, valley tracks, grassy paths and sheep traces over open fells and summit ridges, the route leads through isolated valleys to reservoir shores, tumbling gills, becks and hidden cleuchs in a total height gain of 1634ft/498m. Graded 4, requiring map and compass skills in poor visibility, this delightful route provides challenges without risks and can be completed in 4 hours. Take walking boots and hill equipment to suit the conditions, and as scenic and wildlife interest is high a camera and binoculars are recommended.

ROUTE DIRECTIONS

Coulter village, on the A702(T) road 3 miles / 4.8km south of Biggar, leads via a narrow minor road south, signposted Reservoir, to just beyond Culter Allers Farm by Birthwood House. Limited parking, GR 031311, on the roadside verges prior to or just beyond the bridge and private entrance to Birthwood.

Walk south, by musical Culter Water, on the narrow road with grassy verges into the dark jaws of Culter Water glen for $2^{1/2}$ miles / 4km; watched over by Ward Law and Woodycleuch Dod - **Walk 5**, with their surging gills and dark hidden places, before reaching the dam and outbuildings of Culter Waterhead Reservoir (1). Rise to the dam and keeping to the north shore pass through a gate onto a wide track running east and north above the water's edge. Before long an equally wide track branches left zigzagging the skirts of Knock Hill.

THIS IS THE FIRST OF TWO ALTERNATIVE ROUTES TO THE SUMMIT OF CULTER FELL.

(a) The shooter's track winds north-east over Knock Hill, joining Knock Burn, for $1^{1/2}$ miles / 2.4km to below the summit ridge of Culter Fell, a fading way that eases the ascent of 1240ft/378m. Continue north-east over open fell for the final yards to the guiding fence, raised trig point and its surrounding stones (2).

(b) The second and more adventurous route carries on east then north, with the reservoir inlet, to the mouth of Breeks Burn, where

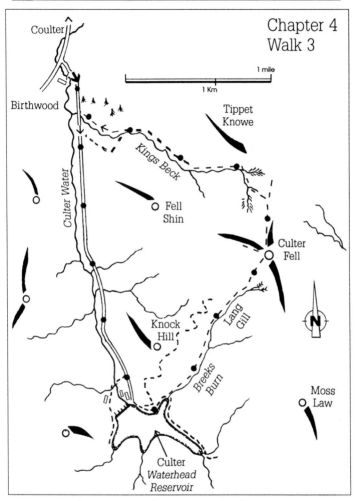

a narrow path ascends into the steep-sided gully on the west side of the burn. Continue north-north-east for ¹/₂ mile / 0.8km to the sheep stell, where three burns meet. Continue ascending by the left watercourse, ie. Lang Gill, as it probes into the very heart of Culter's

177

summit. At the fence it's left to Culter's top and trig point, where the views south over the reservoir compensate for energy expended.

Descend north, left of the guiding fence, for $^1/_2$ mile / 0.8km to the hags of Glenharvie Moss. At the point where the boundary fence swings right, GR 053298, leave it to drop west, ie. left, crossing a twin track and lumpy overgrown hags. Using the conspicuous bulk of Tinto Hill as a marker, on a bearing of 294° magnetic, walk to the north-eastern rim of Kings Beck corrie. As the slope steepens, by the source of a small feeder burn, descend west on the grassy shoulder by this feeder (dry in summer) to its junction with the upper reaches of Kings Beck, flowing in left, through its rocky cleuch, from Culter Fell. At the confluence swing right and descend, on a thin but distinct path, alongside the true right bank of the main burn as it bounds first north then west. At no time is this seemingly steep descent hazardous providing care is taken in foot placement. You meet a grass and dirt track at GR 047299. Follow this vehicle track through the tight glen of Kings Beck, on the true right bank, to just beyond a small settlement tank. Here as it crosses the beck leave the track and continue north-west with Kings Beck, on a dirt path, to meet Culter Water and the plantation with its nide of pheasants. Turn right for the final yards to journey's end by Birthwood.

Accommodation and refreshments in Biggar.

ITEMS OF INTEREST ALONG THE WAY

(1) CULTER WATERHEAD RESERVOIR. Holds approximately 500 million gallons in a lake $^1/_2$ mile / 0.8km wide by $^3/_4$ mile / 1.2km long, and is restrained by a dam with an embankment height of 91ft / 28m. In the latter days of construction, from 1906, the Caledonian Railways splendid new locomotive *Cardean* always blew its "non-standard" whistle each weekday as it approached Symington, 4 miles / 6.4km from Coulter; so precise was *Cardean* it is said workers in the area set their watches by its whistle.

(2) CULTER FELL. From its summit, as from most in the Culter Hills, there is a clear siting to the north-west of the isolated accumulation of Tinto. A mountain as visually dominant as Culter Fell prompted the old, but inaccurate, couplet:

> *Between Tintock Top and Coulter Fell*
> *Bust scarce three handbreadths and an ell.*　　　　Anon

Inaccurate, because an "ell" - a cloth measure equal to $1^{1/4}$yds / 1.15m - (*see Glossary*) plus 12 inches for three handbreadths equals approximately 4.79ft / 1.46m, whereas the actual difference between the two mountains is 135ft / 41m, Culter Fell being the higher. For all that, I still prefer the edict of the old couplet!

WALK 4: Forts, Terraces and Crannog

COULTER - SNAIP - NISBET - COW CASTLE - CRANNOG - LANGLOCH KNOWE - THE CAMP - NISBET - CULTER WATER - COULTER

Flat as the Biggar Gap although not so wide, Kilbucho glen allows the floodwaters of Kilbucho Burn to ebb and flow along Back Ditch either to Tweed or west to Clyde. Low domed hills rise steeply from its flatlands, passing Green Knowe, Crannog, Cow (pronounced 'coo') Castle, Langloch Knowe fort, Camp fort, plus numerous settlements and cultivation terraces. This journey into the distant past wanders for $4^{1/2}$ miles/7.2km around the glen of Kilbucho, beneath Gawky Hill and Scawdmans Law, ascending but a mere 541ft/165m in its travels. Graded an easy 2, it is by grassy path and farm track from waterside to grassy knowe. Wear appropriate clothes/ footwear on this 3 hour search, a delight for the historian, the wildlife enthusiast and all lovers of the outdoors.

A section of the route, not a designated right of way, passes through the arable and pastured property of Nisbet Farm; access to the forts and settlements, via cart tracks and paths, is allowed by courtesy of the owner. I would ask all to observe the country code, particularly during lambing and leave all gates as you found them.

ROUTE DIRECTIONS

Coulter, a small village, lies $2^{1/2}$ miles/4km south from Biggar on the A702(T) and marks the start/finish of the walk. Off-the-road parking, GR 025338, is available north of the school.

Walk south by the school, past the signpost 'Birthwood 2 miles', on a tree-lined lane for $^{1/2}$ mile/0.8km to cross Culter Water at a small bridge below conifer-clad Culter Craigs (1). Immediately beyond the lane forks; take the left, signposted 'Snaip, Nisbet', east alongside Culter Water below the scree of Culter Craigs. Ahead the

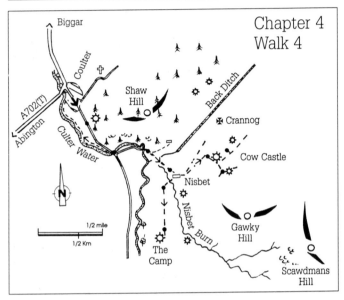

Chapter 4
Walk 4

gravel beds . nd flood plain of Kilbucho glen (2), with Snaip on its small knowe, lead to the elevated, gated and tidy steading of Nisbet.

Pass through the farmyard south-east, ie. left, onto a cart track, swinging left again to forked cart tracks. The left fork leads to the Crannog (3), four fields away, but ends prior to the few remaining crumbling stones - observe it from a distance as its position, not its formation, is of greater interest. The right fork swings, right and left, through a narrow gap to the fort bearing mounds of Cow Castle and Langloch Knowe (4), in addition to an elevated view of the Crannog (3) and surrounding Cultivation Terraces (1). On the higher hillock to the left Cow Castle fort and settlement, ahead and right the fort and 'water heater' on Langloch Knowe (4). Cow Castle provides a fine siting, north over Crannog and flood plain to the Cultivation Terraces on Shaw Hill by Threepland Backshaw (5).

Return to Nisbet steading to cross the ford on Nisbet Burn, and ascend south on a rutted cart track for ½ mile/0.8km, to the raised and grassy foundations of Camp fort (4). A way that provides further sightings of terraces on Bendrie and above by Nisbet Burn, plus the black rocky flanks of Raven Gill on Scawdmans Hill to the east. Retrace your steps via Nisbet and Snaip to cross Culter Water by the outward bridge. Once across pass through the black iron gate in the stone wall onto a pleasing sylvan pathway of $1/2$ mile/0.8km, alongside the burbling Water of Culter, to Coulter village.

Refreshment in Coulter, accommodation and refreshment in Biggar.

ITEMS OF INTEREST ALONG THE WAY

(1) CULTIVATION TERRACES. Four sets of prominent, horizontal contouring terraces surround Nisbet. One, on Culter Craigs, is partially hidden by conifers. Others on the slopes by Bendrie and Langloch Knowe run vertically, ie. 'rig and furrow', but can only be identified from the air. It is likely they were all constructed by monks. Dating is difficult, though they are thought to date from AD 600 to AD 1300.

(2) KILBUCHO GLEN. A name derived from St Bega the virgin, who lived in the area in the 7th century. The present flat-floored glen, to all intents and purposes horizontal for 4 miles/6.4km, is the result of a glacial breach during the Ice Age. From prehistoric to medieval times the floor was submerged in water and scrub, forcing man's passage onto higher drier levels alongside White Hill and Langloch Knowe.

(3) CRANNOG. Centuries ago in the Dark Ages, when the Kilbucho glen was a shallow loch, a fortified defensive tower, known as a Crannog, was built on Green Knowe. Subsequent drainage removed its main defences and today but a few crumbling stones remain.

(4) HILL FORTS. The hill-top forts and settlements date from 3500 BC to AD 300. At Cow Castle and Langloch Knowe the elliptical outer ramparts are clearly visible as they are at the Camp, where foundations of internal buildings are also visible. It is said that a circular water-proofed depression surrounded by cracked and broken rocks, by Langloch Knowe, was used to heat water by placing fired stones within.

(5) THREEPLAND HILL. There is a large hole by Threepland Hill known as the "hole abune Thriepland":

> *Glenkirk & Glencotho,*
> *The Mains o' Kilbucho,*
> *Blendewin & the Raw,*
> *Mitchellhill & the Shaw -*
> *There's a hole abune Thriepland*
> *Wad haud them a'.*

WALK 5: The Hudderstone High Loop

BIRTHWOOD - COWGILL RIG - HUDDERSTONE - WOODYCLEUCH DOD - WARD LAW - HILL END - BIRTHWOOD

*For those who enjoy the solitude and scenery of the Southern Uplands this high-level hike of 7¹/2 miles/12km, over the rolling ridges of the Culter Hills, will provide one of those remembered days. Memories of the glistening waters of Cowgill and Culter Waterhead (1) far below the heights of Cowgill and Woodycleuch Dod, plus sitings of Windgate Bank (**Walk 6**) and the tinted scree of the Diel's Barn Door above Duncan Gill (**Walk 8**). The upward progress totals 1493ft/455m, in four not too severe stages, resulting in a grading of 3, over ridge tracks, thin paths and sheep traces on the open fells; with a stirring final leg of 2 miles/3.2km on the north-bound rig of Woodycleuch Dod (Dod - a domed, ie. without a peak, hill) and Ward Law. Journey time, with boots and mountain gear to suit, approximately 4 hours; that is if you're not too absorbed with the flora, fauna and views along the way.*

ROUTE DIRECTIONS

From Coulter, on the A702(T), a minor road runs 2 miles / 3.2km south to Culter Allers Farm and Birthwood; between which a signposted fork marks the start of the walk to Cowgill reservoir. Limited parking is available on the verges at GR 031311.

Take the right fork leading south by Birthwood Farm, accompanied by the tinkling waters of Hilly Gill and Cow Gill and flanked by the grey scree and occasional tree of Braid Slack on Knowe Dod. Pass the set-back cottage of Windgill before leaving the road left for the gated and clearly visible cart track rising to Cowgill Rig. An ascent that creates casual pauses, which enable the walker to admire the high points of the journey, such as Hudderstone,

Cowgill Upper Reservoir and Tinto ex Hudderstone

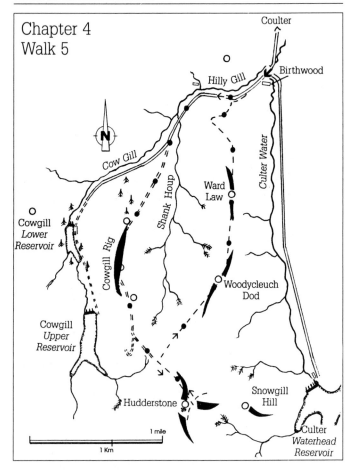

Chapter 4
Walk 5

Woodycleuch Dod and Ward Law, and to slow down the pulse,
before our attention is distracted by the views beyond and below
the rig's cap of conifers. Once over the high point of the rig a short
diversion to the right provides southerly sightings of Cowgill
reservoir, and ahead the deep gouged clefts and gullies, that
epitomise the Culter Hills, of Stotlea Gutter, Yearn Cleuch, Grey

Cowgill Upper Reservoir and curious friends

Side and the Diel's Barn Door (2).

As the rig cart track descends and passes through a gate, veer left with a twin track to meet a guiding fence/wall for a measured ascent of ³/₄ mile/1.2km south-east to the grassy summit of Hudderstone. The views are certainly more outstanding than the tiny cairn (listed on the Pathfinder map as Pile of Stones) marking this Donald's top. After assimilating the views return north-west with the fence of ascent for ¹/₂ mile/0.8km, leaving it with the twin track running north-north-east, ie. right, over the col above Stotlea Gutter and Lea Gill, to Woodycleuch Dod. A clear way, although at certain times of the year wet underfoot, it offers pleasing sights of Lea Gill gully, Culter Waterhead and the hills to the east.

From Woodycleuch Dod the distinct path continues its airy way north, passing Crow Knowes and rounding Ward Law on the western side below the cairned twin top. A diversion to the summit is well worth the little leg-work required, providing as it does a buzzard's-eye view over Hungry Knees of Culter Water glen and beyond, before returning to the track which now descends in a hurry through gates (take care to leave as you found) and pasture to the outward road below Braid Slack by Hilly Gill. Turn right and pass Birthwood, returning to the starting point.

Accommodation and refreshments at Coulter and Biggar.

ITEMS OF INTEREST ALONG THE WAY

(1) RESERVOIRS. The Cowgills were the first of the Culter reservoirs to be built, by the Aidrie and Coatbridge Water Company, under an Act of 1892; the upper of the two was the first project to be contracted by John Best of Edinburgh. The embankment was to be conventional, which meant large quantities of 'puddle clay' were needed to fill the trench in the embankment down to solid rock. This was to cause many problems, ranging from inadequate supplies of quality clay to the transporting of that clay. In 1896 a rail-line was laid and in the Water Company's minutes it is recorded that locomotives were to be used, but Best used horses as well. The supply line was in use from May 1896 to the end of 1898, with constant problems. In 1899 the valve was finally closed and the lake was filled, only to be emptied in spring 1900 because of dirty water; after the refill in July 1900, Best's account of £40,000 was settled.

Work on the lower reservoir was started in 1900 by David Waddell and completed in 1903, a period dogged by a disaster-prone traction engine, which ran away on Snaip Brae (**Walk 4**). The steersman fell off but the 67-year-old driver, John Moarfoot, steered the engine into a field without overturning. In May 1901 the steersman was killed in an accident at the bridge near Birthwood House when the engine overturned and fell 10 feet into a stream, with driver Moarfoot suffering extensive burns and bruises. It was suggested the steersman had fallen asleep, having been at a dance the night before.

(2) DIEL'S BARN DOOR. At GR 002263, on the north-west ridge of Whitelaw Brae, a slash of scree above Duncan Gill and also on the west side of the ridge by the source of Wandel Burn.

WALK 6: The Windgate Gap & Kyegill Slop:

BIRTHWOOD - COWGILL RIG - WINDGATE BANK - HUDDERSTONE - SNOWGILL HILL - CULTER WATERHEAD - CULTER WATER GLEN - BIRTHWOOD

An up and down circular walk of 9 miles/14.4km, ascending 1526ft/465m in total as the route rises, providing a rich mix of heather-splashed fell and glen that typifies these tight packed hills. The grading of 3 is justified as the way travels over sections of demanding terrain, covering practically the entire spectrum of below-soles conditions, through the heart of the Culter Hills. Wear appropriate clothes and footwear, take map and compass and a good pair of lungs together with a camera and an eager step and you won't be disappointed. A 5 hour way, rich in the life of the Southern Upland fells.

ROUTE DIRECTIONS

Start between Culter Allers Farm and Birthwood, 2 miles/3.2km south from Coulter village (A702) via a minor road, where limited roadside parking is available, GR 031311.

At the fork follow the signposted lane, 'Cowgill Reservoirs', south-west and west with the musical waters of Hilly Gill and Cow Gill for 1 mile/1.6km. A way that quickly enfolds the walker, once past Birthwood Farm, in the steep stony slopes of Braid Slack and Windgill Knowe before leaving the lane left to ascend a gated cart track rising to tree-topped Cowgill Rig. The initial climb is a bit of a plod to the wind-blown conifers but once there this 2 mile/1.6km ridge rewards the walker tenfold. At every point, both near and far, are views of mountain form that must surely please and invite; in particular Cowgill Upper reservoir (1) below the immediate black hills, rent assunder with cleuchs scored and split as if by the mad hand of a primordial axe-man. And all this with the accompanying song of lark and whaup.

As the track descends, and the black bulk of Hudderstone looms ahead, pass through a gate for a sharp zigzag down to the green valley floor, above Cowgill reservoir, and below the crumbling stone and sheep pens of Windgate House. Once on the valley floor ascend south-east by the grassy banks of Fair Burn, passing Yearn Cleuch, into the steep-sided cleft below Windgate Bank's scree slopes and protruding rocks, leading to the high, gated bealach

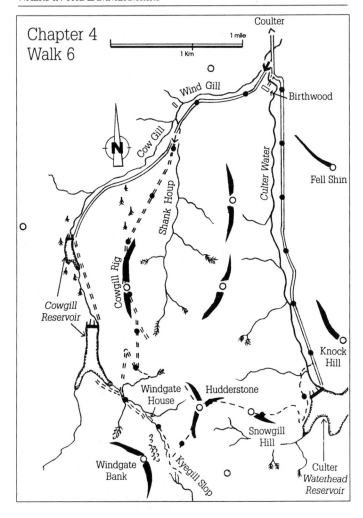

Chapter 4
Walk 6

1 mile

1 Km

Coulter

Wind Gill

Birthwood

Cow Gill

Fell Shin

Shank Houp

Culter Water

Cowgill Rig

Cowgill
Reservoir

Knock
Hill

Windgate
House

Hudderstone

Snowgill
Hill

Windgate
Bank

Kyegill Slop

Culter
Waterhead
Reservoir

quaintly known as Kyegill Slop; a height gain of 600ft/140m. On reaching the narrow but appropriately named col, with its covering of moorland soup, do not be tempted by a scramble over the

188

adjacent naked rock - IT IS FLAKY AND UNSTABLE. The col does however provide fine sightings north-west, over Cowgill Upper reservoir, of Tinto's massive bulk.

Ascend Hudderstone's steep and heathery shoulder north-east and north, keeping left of the fence, where fine grass signals the final yards to Hudderstone's (2) summit marked by a sad 'pile of stones'. Leave the summit fence at its right angle for a gentle descent east over the broad connecting ridge to nearby Snowgill Hill. And as befits this western bastion of Culter Waterhead reservoir (3), it provides fine views of the glistening waters below and Culter Fell beyond, in addition to the steep-sided cleuchs and the craigs of Snow Gill. Tracks lead down the rounded eastern and north-eastern slopes to join a cart track crossing Culter Water by a bridge, below the grassy slopes of Culter Waterhead dam.

The final 2 miles/3.2km are through the narrow glen of Culter Water, on the grassy verges of the reservoir road, overlooked by Woodycleuch Dod (named after long-gone trees), Ward Law (**Walk 5**), Knock Hill and Fell Shin (**Walks 3 & 2**). Journey's end is marked by the old beeches that line the Water of Culter by Birthwood.

Accommodation and refreshments available in Coulter and Biggar.

ITEMS OF INTEREST ALONG THE WAY

(1) COWGILL RESERVOIRS. An essential item in the construction of the two Cowgill reservoirs was that of transportation, in particular vast quantities of 'puddle clay' for the huge embankments. For this purpose rail proved less troublesome than road, and the rail bed at the start of a narrow gauge line, early 1896, that led to Cowgill Upper reservoir, can be seen near to the commencement of the ascent of Cowgill Rig. The roads in Cow Gill valley were so narrow one traction engine could not pass another, and as a result "38 wagons of clay were piled up at Carstairs Junction".

(2) HUDDERSTONE. Previously known as Heatherstane Law, for reasons that are obvious now the hill has been traversed. It and its neighbours maintain a blanced, if not harmonious, population of grouse, peewit, curlew, lark, stone chat, buzzard and hen harrier in addition to a thriving husk of mad mountain hares.

(3) CULTER WATERHEAD RESERVOIR. From Snowgill Hill a bird's-eye view could reveal the layout of the narrow gauge lines

that threaded across the northern slopes of the enbankment to connect with the supply line running up from Coulter. A line that ran between today's road and Culter Water, carrying 10 loads of clay per day in early 1905, with a locomotive shed close to the farm track that crosses Culter Water from the shepherd's cottage to join the roadway. North of this track, between road and water, stood the 'hutted camp'.

WALK 7: A Circuit of Camps Reservoir

CAMPS WATER - CAMPS DAM - FALL CLEUCH WOOD - GRAINS - CAMPS KNOWE & KNEESEND WOODS - CAMPS WATER - CAMPS DAM

A 5½ mile/8.8km circuit along the shoreline track of the three-legged reservoir of Camps; a restful journey rich in wildlife, in particular water and moorland birds, set in a quiet corner of the Culter Hills. Graded 1 with an unnoticed height gain of 131ft/40m, the entire walk is on hard-core roads with a short section of grassy tree-lined pathway. Good trainers or lightweight walking boots will suffice. Caution is needed should shoreline timber felling be in progress and walkers are requested to keep to the route described and to observe Strathclyde Water Services' notices.

ROUTE DIRECTIONS

Access to the approaches of Camps reservoir (1), GR 985222, is gained via a narrow road, with passing places, along Camps Water valley 3 miles / 4.8km east of Crawford (2), a village overlooking the upper Clyde alongside the old A74 and close to the new M74. Limited roadside parking, GR 985222, 1 mile / 1.6km west of Camps dam, is on a layby at the gated corner of the plantation covering Great Hill; take care not to obstruct access to the forest road.

Walk east with the road, above the horseshoes of Camp Water, and as the green slopes of the dam come into view take the left fork, descending past the houses and Strathclyde Water Services buildings. At the end house swing right and then left to enter the conifers on a narrow grassy path ascending to the southern end of the dam, where a stile leads onto the tarmac road across the dam. At the northern end the way swings right by the overflow, ie. east, and

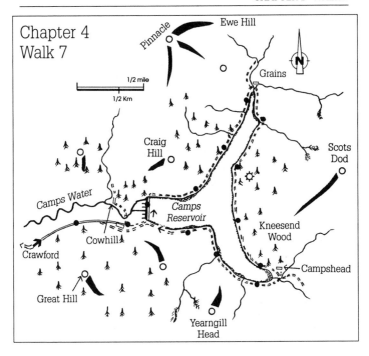

Chapter 4
Walk 7

Pinnacle

Ewe Hill

Grains

Craig Hill

Scots Dod

Camps Water

Camps Reservoir

Kneesend Wood

Cowhill

Crawford

Campshead

Great Hill

Yearngill Head

1/2 mile

1/2 Km

north-east on a wide road contouring Craig Hill and the conifers of Fall Cleuch Wood.

Now completely enclosed by the sloping flanks of the surrounding hills our path continues, alongside the narrow northerly finger of the reservoir, to the house of Grains at the confluence of Grains Burn, from the north, and Whitelaw Burn, from the east. The way swings right, at the head of the reservoir, to pass the steading of Grains - note the conical grass-covered hill (3) rising left, ie. between Robert Cleuch and Howe Cleuch. Beyond the sheep pens the journey south begins, 1¹/₂ miles / 2.4kms of ever changing views, passing Martin Cleuch with its water-washed gullies on the flanks of Scots Dod clearly visible. Next Camps Knowe Wood and Casan Cleuch, above which the remains of a prehistoric fort stand, are passed leading to the south-east finger of Camps reservoir. As the way curves left, below the pines of Kneesend Wood, a grass track forks left to a disused quarry. Here a narrow path continues through the trees parallel with the shoreline road and rejoining the road by a gate and noticeboard. Pass by the house at Campshead before crossing the bridge over Camps Water at this damp extremity of the reservoir.

The final leg winds west, north and west again with the shoreline below the watchful gaze of cleuch-scarred Midge Hill and Reeve Hill from the south. The views to the north reveal glimpses of the dome of Hudderstone over the flashing colours of screeching oyster catchers (4) as they noisily rise from the water's edge. At the dam continue with the wide conifer-lined road as it angles above the white reservoir buildings to pass through a gate (please ensure it is closed) to join the outward road below Great Hill and above winding Camps Water.

ITEMS OF INTEREST ALONG THE WAY

(1) CAMPS RESERVOIR. The largest and most recent reservoir in the Culter Hills. At 1070ft/326m above sea level it was instigated by Lanarkshire Water Orders between 1913 and 1920. Unlike most waterworks schemes, construction at Camps was not held up by the Great War; indeed German POWs commenced work on 22 August 1916, their numbers rising to 220 in February 1917. One of the sidings on the approach rail line, Schneider's Cutting or Loop by Normangill, was named after the POW who built it. However work slowed when the POWs departed and it was not until May 1930 that the formal inauguration occurred.

(2) CRAWFORD. Bronze Age, Iron Age man and Roman (Watling Street) have walked this way, as did William Wallace and James V. The remains of Crawford Castle, known as Lindsay Tower, can be seen by Camps Water; today it is fenced off as a dangerous ruin. Nearby the upper Clyde flows by, prompting Burns to pen,

> *Yon wild mossy mountains sae lofty and wide,*
> *That nurse in their bosom the youth o' the Clyde*

(3) PINNACLE. This conspicuous shoulder, above Grains, marking the end of Pinnacle's south-east ridge, appears the more likely candidate to bear the name Pinnacle than the flat fell above. Could

the topographers in centuries past have named the wrong hill?

(4) OYSTER CATCHER. Also known as mussel-pickers, these large waders 'nest' where adequate stretches of shingle are available, to camouflage eggs and downy chicks without fear of detection. A noisy, colourful bird, black and white with an elongated orange beak, it deafens the waterways with its shrill shrieks, all day and often through the night.

WALK 8: The Diel's Barn Door

CAMPS WATER - CRAIG HILL - PINNACLE - WHITELAW BRAE - DIEL'S BARN DOOR - THREE GRAINS - GRAINS BURN - CAMPS RESERVOIR & DAM

A visit to the largest of the Culter reservoirs, Camps reservoir, and by the lonely hills beyond to the mystery of the Diel's Barn Door. The approach from Crawford on the western perimeter of the Culter Hills offers a circular walk of 9 miles/14.4km on forest and reservoir tracks and open fell pathways. This grade 3 hill walk of 4$^{1/2}$ hours, with a height gain of 1302ft/ 397m, is steep initially but well worth the effort, for not only does the route open up fine views of the range but also the way is rich in wildlife and items of interest. Walking boots, correct clothing, map/compass are needed and a camera/binoculars will enlighten the journey.

ROUTE DIRECTIONS
From Crawford, on the A74, a narrow road crosses the winding Clyde and beyond the ruins of Castle Crawford travels east for 1$^{1/2}$ miles / 2.4km alongside Camps Water (1). At GR 985222 1 mile / 1.6km west of Camps reservoir, at the gated corner of the conifer-covered Great Hill, off-road parking is available on the layby; do not restrict forest access.

Walk east with the road, forking left, then beyond the reservoir buildings swing left to cross Camps Water to Cowhill standing by Swine Gill. Prior to Cowhill leave the farm road with a pathway to the north-western corner of a conifer stand rising steeply to Craig Hill. A dirt and grass path climbs east, leaving the trees to reach the summit of Craig Hill and the tree-line of Fall Cleuch Wood. On the

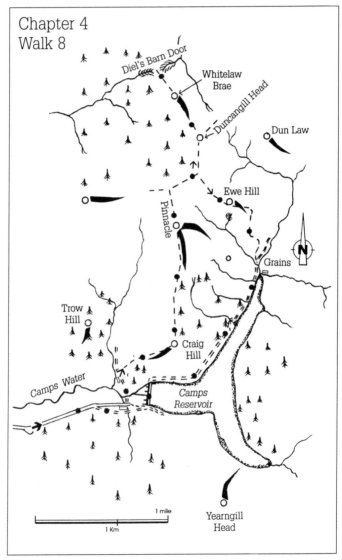

Chapter 4
Walk 8

Diel's Barn Door

Whitelaw Brae

Duncangill Head

Dun Law

Ewe Hill

Pinnacle

Grains

Trow Hill

Craig Hill

Camps Water

Camps Reservoir

N

1 mile

1 Km

Yearngill Head

ridge north to Pinnacle, at times wet underfoot, the tree-line provides a guide rising with the ridge, ie. for half the way, to the flat and undistinguished summit of Pinnacle.

Continue due north for $^1/_2$ mile/0.8km to an angled post and wire fence, turn right and follow the fence, through heather and tussock, to the next angle swinging due north to a three-fence junction on the bleak expanse of Duncangill Head. West twists the conifer-clad narrow valley of Birnock Burn, east the watershed between Windgate Bank and Dun Law, and ahead, ie. north-north-west, a fence leads over the trig point of Whitelaw Brae to the Diel's Barn Door (2). The cleuchs of this distinct phenomenon, below both sides of the col, are to be given a wide berth and observed from a safe distance. Whitelaw Brae, a bump in the ridge, offers extensive vistas over the entire Culter range, especially north, through the confines of Duncan Gill to the reservoirs of Cowgill and north-east to Culter Fell.

Return with the outward fence to Duncangill Head and continue south for $^3/_4$ mile/1.2km to the angled point where the fence swings south-west. At this angle leave the fence and connect with a twin track running east-south-east just below the summit of the grass and heather ridge traversing Ewe Hill, high above the narrow north wall of Howe Cleuch. The way runs a few feet below the top of Ewe Hill before swinging east and descending on a choice of tracks and traces that wind down south-east to cross Grains Burn and join the reservoir road at Grains inlet. An alternative descent, to the reservoir road, would be to continue descending the outward route from the fence via Pinnacle to the northern tip of Fall Cleuch Wood. Then follow the northern woodside fence, south-east and east to Camps reservoir, joining the road via a wooden wicket gate.

Continue south and west, with the roadway, by Fall Cleuch Wood and below Craig Hill; a way of pleasant contrasts with Midge Hill and Yearngill Hill rising solidly above the glistening waters of Camps. Pass a quarry (3) to reach the reservoir's weir and spillway, swinging right with the tarmac road over the top of the dam. Continue right via the forest road, leading west (by the site of the reservoir's 'hutted camp') to the fork onto the roadway, to our starting point below Great Hill.

Accommodation and refreshments at Crawford and Abington.

ITEMS OF INTEREST ALONG THE WAY

(1) CAMPS WATER. Interesting though the construction of Camps reservoir was, I feel its original infrastructure of road and rail deserves a mention. In September 1916 the materials for a temporary 3ft gauge line, covering the $3^1/2$ miles/5.6km from the Caledonian Railway at Crawford to Camps on a widened road, were assembled. Later plans were changed and a new road was built south of the existing one, with a more substantial 3ft gauge railway; both were to all intents completed in 1919. A fine stone three-span bridge crossing the Clyde from Crawford station sidings carried the narrow gauge line to Camps. Today the stone piers remain but carry a footbridge only. Also rail beds, remains of water tanks and old road routes can be distinguished alongside today's road.

Lanarkshire County Council built Camps with direct labour and owned all the plant; the main reservoir rail line remained in situ until 1940, finally dismantled by the auctioneer's hammer of Smellie and Sons, Hamilton.

(2) DIEL'S BARN DOOR. *Diel* is Scots for devil. This dramatic slash, GR 002263, on both sides of the col between Hardrigg Head and Whitelaw Brae is, in technical terms, a cranny between a rocky overhang and a deteriorated tor. In reality, it is a pink scree scar of great steepness high above Duncan Gill and by the source of Wandel Burn.

(3) QUARRY. The main quarry for rough stone, still retained, stood above a stone shute and crusher by a narrow gauge line. A line linked by other lines to excavators, the east bank quarry and the main embankment.

WALK 9: Culter Water Glen & Kingledoors Ridge

COULTER VILLAGE - BIRTHWOOD - CULTER WATER GLEN & RESERVOIR - HOLM NICK - GATHERSNOW HILL - COOMB HILL - GLENLOOD HILL - GLENCOTHO - HOLMS WATER

A linear walk of $11^3/4$ miles/18.8km that will require transport should the journey end in Glenholm, ie. Holms Water glen. Scenically pleasing, with both near and distant views, it is well worth the, at times laborious, height

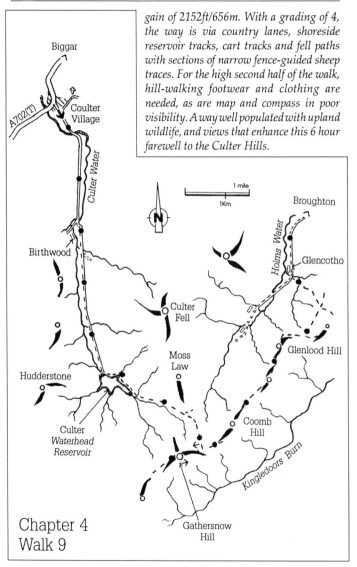

gain of 2152ft/656m. With a grading of 4, the way is via country lanes, shoreside reservoir tracks, cart tracks and fell paths with sections of narrow fence-guided sheep traces. For the high second half of the walk, hill-walking footwear and clothing are needed, as are map and compass in poor visibility. A way well populated with upland wildlife, and views that enhance this 6 hour farewell to the Culter Hills.

Biggar

Coulter Village

A702(T)

Culter Water

Birthwood

Hudderstone

Culter Waterhead Reservoir

1 mile

1Km

N

Broughton

Holms Water

Glencotho

Culter Fell

Moss Law

Glenlood Hill

Coomb Hill

Kingledoors Burn

Gathersnow Hill

Chapter 4
Walk 9

ROUTE DIRECTIONS

Coulter village lines both Culter Water and the busy A702(T) road, some 2$^{1/2}$ miles/4km south of the market town of Biggar and 1 mile/ 1.6km east of the River Clyde at the west end of the Biggar Gap. Off-road parking is available just north of Coulter school - take care not to block access. The walk could be started near Birthwood (as in **Walks 2 & 3**), shortening the route by 2 miles/3.2km, although in the author's opinion this amputation changes the character and restricts the varying landscapes of this grand finale to the Culter Hills.

Walk south, signposted 'Birthwood 2 miles', from Coulter school with the ever narrowing lane curving below the conifers and cultivation terraces of Culter Craigs. Once across Craigend Bridge over Culter Water take the right fork to the reservoirs on Birthwood Road, a road that climbs due south above the windings and flood plain of Culter Water by Snaip (1).

This stretch to Culter Allers Farm and Birthwood, although over tarmac, provides enticing views of the approaching black flanks of Culter Fell and its outlyers. Beyond Culter Allers Farm and before the private entrance to Birthwood, take the left fork to Culter Waterhead reservoir (spellings of Culter/Coulter vary in the OS Landranger and Pathfinder maps), a southbound lane that penetrates Culter Water glen, below the sombre sides of Ward Law, Fall Shin, Woodycleuch Dod and Knock Hill, before reaching the heavy grass-clad embankment of the reservoir.

At the dam pass the dam-keeper's house and through a gate to the track alongside the north shore, winding by Breeks Burn and Bucht Slack to the sheep pens at the eastern extremity. From this track and the subsequent rise to Holm Nick the massive bulk of Culter Fell and Moss Law are unseen, south and west a moonscape of dark and heavy hills rent asunder by the shaley cleuchs and gullies that are the hallmark of the Culters.

Swing left through a gate, rising with Culter Water past a conifer stand, on a stony track winding east-south-east for 1 mile/1.6km to the col and watershed of Holm Nick (2); this track and surrounds are dour, yet all have fascinating names - Bramble Sike, Suckler Grain, Peat Rig, Lang Grain and the rocks of Nout Craig. An escape route, if required, follows Holms Water north-north-east, descending

1³/₄ miles/2.8km to the cottage of Holms Waterhead. Just prior to the gated fence on Holm Nick swing right, ie. south-east, past the carrion crow trap (3) with a reducing grassy track that ascends east and south with the fence to the summit of that prominent watershed Gathersnow Hill (4); fine underfoot and a grandstand of repute.

The departure east, from the grassy summit of Gathersnow, marks the start of a 3¹/₂ mile/5.6km roller-coaster of a ridge walk to beyond Cocklie Rig Head. Involving a height gain of 597ft/182m over four summits the tedium of ascent is soon forgotten as seldom-seen sights of Tweeddale's skyline and close-ups of Culter Fell and Chapelgill across Holms Water explode into view. At the fence junction on Glenwhappen Rig, continue north-east with another fence, over the rig to Coomb Hill, marked by an untidy pile of stones and a fence post. Underfoot, the way is by narrow fenceside traces or twin tracks west of the fence. Continue over the heathery flanks of Broomy Law and Glenlood Hill, beyond whose summit track and fence descend sharp right, ie. east, to the col above the naked cleuch of Glencotho Burn.

From the col follow a grassy twin track, rutted in places, north and north-north-east for ¹/₂ mile/0.8km as it contours through heather to a grass-clad clearing above a feeder burn, GR 091293, descending into Glencotho Burn by the sheep stell below. As the grass gives way to heather a faint twin track can be seen left, becoming more distinct as a fence is approached and a rocky outcrop is seen. Follow this path, by slip rails and a footbridge, to the conifers and in-bye pastures of Glencotho and the glen road by Holms Water - journey's end. Please note that at Glencotho, and all Culter farms, sheep are of prime importance. Respect the countryside and its practices and at lambing in April and early May avoid the area. At other times keep to the paths, close all gates and leave your dog at home.

Should transport not be available the Holms Water road leads north-east to the A701 and Broughton, a delightful valley walk; regretfully it will add 4¹/₂ miles/7.2km to your journey.

Accommodation and refreshments in Broughton and Biggar.

ITEMS OF INTEREST ALONG THE WAY

(1) SNAIP. Site of a standard gauge rail line that ran from Coulter

village (through what is now the school) via Snaip to Culter Allers Farm and then to Culter Waterhead in the early 1900s. A supply line for the reservoir contractors, it crossed Culter Water below Craigend Bridge and had a long 'lye' (siding) for crossing or stabling trains by Snaip Farm, turning up into the valley by an acute bend below Snaip. At Snaip Brae a traction engine ran out of control into a field.

(2) HOLM NICK. A pass and watershed, from where Culter Water flows into the Clyde and thence into the Irish Sea; whilst Holms Water trickles merrily north to Tweed and the North Sea.

(3) CARRION CROWS. A sizeable post and wire netting trap, approved by the RSPB and the NCC, is set on Holm Nick to capture carrion crows. Birds who rob nests of eggs and chicks and have been known to take the eyes from sheep and lambs. Please leave the trap as you found it.

(4) GATHERSNOW HILL. At 2257ft/688m a mountain of some presence, albeit little eye appeal; it nevertheless can be seen from afar, this grass and heather watershed. Aptly named, its many gullies, cleuchs and depressions, particularly on its northern slopes, hold snow-eggs well into the month of May giving a steady water supply to Clyde via Culter Water and Fingland Burn, and Tweed via another Fingland Burn and the two burns of Cule.

Views are extensive and pleasing, not only of the reservoirs of Fruid and Talla to the south and Culter Water north, but also more distant Tinto and the tower-bearing Lowther Hills to the south-west. A good place to have a mid-journey break.

GLOSSARY

LOCAL TERMS AND NAMES

Abune - About, around

Bannock - A rich fruit confection

Bield - Shelter, from the elements

Blaeberry - Bilberry, small edible purple berry

Brake - Broke or destroyed

Brig - Bridge

Burn - Small stream

Cadger - Itinerant packman or carrier/medieval travelling salesman

Cartulary - Monastery register-book

Cist - Stone coffin or burial box

Clag - Scotch mist, low clinging cloud

Clatchy - Muddy, clarty

Cleikin - To hook or spear

Cleuch - Narrow gully with burn; English spelling Cleugh

Col - High saddle or bealach

Collie - Border sheep dog

Corrie - Glaciated hollow in mountainside, cirque

Craig - Rocky outcrop or crag

Culter - An obsolete form of Coulter - Fore-iron of a plough share

Diel - Devil (Scots)

Dod - Local synonym for the name George; or a flat domed hill-top

Dolmen - Two upright stones supporting a flat stone

Dominie - School master (Scots)

Donalds - Mountains between 2000 and 2499ft, list prepared by Percy Donald

Donjon - Strong central tower of an ancient castle

Dreich - Long, tiresome, as on a wet day

Drumlins - Glacial deposit in the form of a small hillock

Doune - Down

Dune - Done

Dyke - Dry stone wall, or man-made trench

Ell - Measure of length originally taken from the arm. A cloth measure equal to $1\frac{1}{4}$ yards

Eskers - Ridged glacial debris (Norse)

Feral - Wild, descended from domestic stock, as in goat or mink

Gaed - Went

Gait - Medieval, road or path

Gauger - 18th century Customs & Excise man

Gimmer - Sheep, ewe

Gill - Burn (common Pennine name)

Glar - Mud

Grain - Rushing burn (Norse)

Grange - Granary (Fr), farm associated with an abbey settled by French monks

Haud - Hold

Haugh - Flat ground by water

Herd - Shepherd

Heugh - Sharp-ended hill

Hoary - Grey with age

Hope - Sheltered valley or glen

Idiograph - Trademark or hallmark

Ilk - The same, a name the same as an ancestral estate

Ilka - Every (Scots)

Isoclinal lines - Three classes of phenomena or geological

Jougs - A chained iron neck-ring to restrain felons

Kames - Glacial debris in ridges

Keepted - Kept

Lammas - 1st August, the feast of the first-fruits

Lapwing - Plover or peewit

Law - Hill

Leat - Water running to a mill

Linn - Waterfall or -slide

Loch - Lake

Lochan - Small lake

Maike - Every (Scots)

Mercat -	Market	Spake -	Spoke
Mosstrooper -	Civic guard or reiver	Steading -	Farm buildings/yard
Nae -	No	Stell -	Stone sheep shelter - round,
Nide -	Collective noun for pheasants		rectangular or occasionally
Peewit -	Plover		hexagonal
Peth -	(plural Peaths), path or pathway	Swire -	A neck of land
	(old Scots)	Tane -	One/ones
Quaff -	To drink in large draughts	Thin -	when referring to wind -
Reiver -	Blackmailing cattle thief or		penetrating or cutting
	Border hero	Tithers -	Others
Rig -	Ridge (Local spelling, in England	Trows -	Small valleys
	it is invariably spelt Rigg)	Trudge -	A weary walk
Rill -	Small burn	Tryst -	Meeting or place of meeting
Rodes -	Roads or tracks (medieval)	Tup -	Sheep, entire male/ram
Sae -	So	Wad -	Would
Scotsman's Heid -	Cotton grass	Waddin' -	Wedding
Shiel -	Summer grazing on high ground	Wedder -	Castrated ram/tup
Shieling -	Small shelter on summer grazing	Whaup -	Curlew
Sike -	also Syke, a Burn	Yett -	Gate or door (Scots)

BIBLIOGRAPHY

August in Skye, Ross and Sutherland by Reverend T. Ratcliffe Barnett, R. Grant & Son, Edinburgh, 1930.

The Birds of Berwickshire by George Muirhead, David Douglas, Edinburgh, 1895.

Border Byeways & Lothian Lore by Reverend T. Ratcliff Barnett, R. Grant & Son, Edinburgh, 6th Edition, 1950.

The Borders by F. R. Banks, B. T. Batsford Ltd, London, 1977.

Brave Borderland by H. Drummond Gauld, Thomas Nelson & Sons Ltd. No date.

Bride of Lammermoor by Walter Scott, Oxford University Press, 1991.

Fast Castle The Early Years by Mary Kennaway, Edinburgh Archaeological Field Society, 1992.

The Gateway to Scotland by Bradley, Constable, 1912.

The Glamour of the Glen by Wm McConachie, Oliver and Boyd, Edinburgh, 1930.

Glimpses into the Past in Lammermuir by J. H. Browne, editor N. Mcleish, Alba Publishing, Hawick, 1992.

A Guide to Prehistoric Scotland by R. W. Feachan, B. T. Batsford Ltd, 1963.

Fragments of Scottish History by Sir J. G. Dalyell, 'The Expedicion into Scotlande', 1798.

Highways & Byeways: In The Border by Andrew & John Lang, Macmillan & Co, 1913; reprint 1914 & 1929.

History of Peeblesshire, Vol 1, 11, 111 edited by J. W. Buchan, Jackson, Wylie & Co, Glasgow, 1927.

Lothian Walks by D. G. Moir, Bartholemew, 1939.

More Old Roads in the Lammermuirs by Angus Graham, Proceedings of the Society of Antiquaries of Scotland, pages 217-235, 1959-1960.

Edins Hall Broch on Cockburnlaw, on the Lammermoor Hills by John Stuart, Proceedings of the Society of Antiquaries of Scotland, pages 41-47, 1868.

On Foot, In Southern Scotland by Terry Marsh, David and Charles, Devon, 1995.

One Hundred Hill Walks Around Edinburgh by Chalmers and Storey, Mainstream Publishing, 1990.

Portrait of the Lothians by Nigel Tranter, Robert Hale, London, 1979.

The Roads of Mediaeval Lauderdale by R. P. Hardy, Oliver & Boyd, Edinburgh, 1942.

The Royal Commission on the Ancient and Historical Monuments & Constructions of Scotland. Inventory for the County of Berwick - No 115, pages 60 to 64, 1915.

Scottish Hill Tracks 1. Southern Scotland by D. G. Moir, Albyn Press, 1947. Bartholemew 1975.

The Southern Uplands by Andrew & Thripleton, The Scottish Mountaineering Trust, 1972, recent edition by K. M. Andrew.

The Southern Upland Way by Roger Smith, HMSO, 1994.

Notes on Seven Lammermoor Roads by Angus Graham, Berwickshire Naturalists' Club, Volume 35 (page 288), 1959-1961.

USEFUL INFORMATION

ACCOMMODATION

Lists and bookings together with a Book-a-Bed Ahead scheme, plus details of transport, border abbeys, castles, ancient monuments, museums and galleries, visitor centres, gardens, crafts, leisure and recreation, and 'What's On' can be obtained from the tourist information centres listed below: -

Scottish Borders Tourist Board

Coldstream, High Street, open April-October -	(01890) 882607
Eyemouth, Auld Kirk, open April-October -	(018907) 50678
Galashiels, 3 St John' Street, open April-October -	(01896) 755551
Hawick, Drumlanrig's Tower, open all year -	(01450) 372547
Jedburgh, Murrays Green, open all year -	(01835) 863435/863688
Kelso, Town House, open April-October -	(01573) 223464
Melrose, Abbey House, open April-October -	(01896) 822555
Peebles, High Street, open Easter-end November -	(01721) 720138
Selkirk, Halliwells House, open April-October -	(01750) 20054

East Lothian Tourist Board

Dunbar, 143 High Street -	(01368) 863353
Haddington, Pencraig, A1 by Haddington -	(01620) 860063

Midlothian Tourism

Dalkeith, Dalkeith Library, White Hart Street -	(0131) 663 2083
	(0131) 660 6818
Penicuik, Edinburgh Crystal Visitor Centre, Eastfield, open Easter-October -	(01968) 673846

Clyde Valley Tourist Board

Abington, Welcome Break, Motorway Service Area, open all year -	(01864) 602436
Biggar, 155 High Street, open Easter-October -	(01899) 21066

Dumfriesshire Tourist Board

Moffat, Churchgate, open April-October -	(01683) 20620

Northumbria Tourist Board

Berwick-upon-Tweed, Castlegate -	(01289) 330733

Scottish Youth Hostels

Abbey St Bathans, Duns, open 15/5-29/10 -	(01361) 840245
Broadmeadows, Selkirk, open 29/3-30/9 -	(01750) 76262
Coldingham, The Mount, Coldingham, open 29/3-30/9 -	(018907) 71298
Melrose, Priorwood, Melrose, open 1/3-30/9 -	(01896) 822521
Snoot, Roberton, Hawick, open 29/3-30/9 -	(01450) 880559
Wanlockhead, Lotus Lodge, Biggar -	(01659) 74252

TRANSPORT
Air
Edinburgh International Airport, Turnhouse, Edinburgh - (0131) 333 1000
Newcastle International Airport, Woolsington, Newcastle - (0191) 286 0966

Rail
British Rail, Berwick-upon-Tweed -	(01289) 306771
Scot Rail, Waverley Station, Edinburgh -	(0131) 556 2477
British Rail, Carlisle -	(01228) 44711
Scot Rail, Lockerbie -	(01576) 202637

Road, Long Distance
National Express Ltd, Galloway Coach Station, Newcastle-upon-Tyne -
(0191) 261 9727
Scottish Citylink Coaches Ltd, Buchanan Bus Station, Killermont Street,

Glasgow	(0141)332 919
Edinburgh	(0131) 557 5717
London	(0171) 636 9373
Galashiels	(01896) 752237

Local Services
Timetables and fare details available from:
Director of Roads and Transportation, Scottish Borders Council

Newton St Boswells, Melrose, TD6 OSA -	(01835) 824000
Berwick-upon-Tweed Bus Station, Main Street, Berwick	
Lowland Scottish -	(01289) 307461
East Lothian Tourist Board, 31 Court Street, Haddington -	(01620) 827422
Midlothian Tourism Board, 2 Clerk Street, Loanhead -	(0131) 440 2210
Clyde Valley Tourist Board, Horsemarket, Lanark -	(01555) 662544

Plus local bus stations and tourist information centres listed above.

MISCELLANEOUS ADDRESSES:
Countryside Commission for Scotland, Battleby, Redgorton, Perth PH1 3EW

Countryside Ranger Service, Scottish Borders Council, Newtown St Boswells, Melrose TD6 0SA

East Lothian District Council, Countryside Ranger Service, Haddington, East Lothian

Forestry Commission Headquarters, 231 Corstorphine Road, Edinburgh EH12 7AT

Historic Scotland, 20 Brandon Place, Edinburgh EH3 5RA

Mountaineering Council of Scotland, National Officer, Flat 1R, 71 King Street, Crieff, Perthshire PH7 3HB

National Trust for Scotland, 158 Ingram Street, Glasgow G1 1EJ

Nature Conservancy Council, Archbold House, Archbold Terrace, Newcastle-upon-Tyne NE2 1EG

Ordnance Survey, Romsey Road, Maybush, Southampton SO9 4DH; a range of local OS maps available from local outdoor shops and newsagents

Ramblers Association, 1/5, Wandsworth Road, London SW8 2LJ

Royal Society for the Protection of Birds, The Lodge, Sandy, Beds SG19 2DL

Scottish Natural Heritage, 3 Market Street, Galashiels, Scottish Borders

Scottish Rights of Way Society, John Cotton Business Centre, 10/2 Sunnyside, Edinburgh EH7 5RA

Scottish Youth Hostels Association, 7 Glebe Crescent, Stirling FK8 2JA

Strathclyde Water Services, 419 Balmore Road, Glasgow G22 6NU. (0141) 3555333

Woodland Trust, Westgate, Grantham, Lincs NG31 6LL

Youth Hostels Association, Trevelyan House, St Albans, Herts AL1 2DY

Mountain Rescue Services/Police - Freephone 999
Borders General Hospital, Melrose, Roxburghshire. (01896) 824333.

WEATHER FORECASTS:

(1)	Glasgow Weather Centre, for the Southern Uplands -	(0141) 248 3451
(2)	Edinburgh Meteorological Office, Edinburgh Weather Centre -	(0131) 244 8362/8363
(3)	Mountain Call, Eastern Borders -	(01898) 500 422
(4)	Weather Watchers, any area -	(016445) 652 4239
(5)	Daily forecasts, Radio Borders FM 96.8 -	
(6)	Daily forecasts, Border Television, Teletext -	page 105
(7)	Daily forecasts, BBC Radio Scotland FM 93.5 -	0855/1255 hours

Hill Walkers forecast Friday/Saturday,
BBC Radio Scotland FM 93.5 - 1930/0703 hours

(8)	Monday/Friday, BBC TV Scotland -	1855 hours
(9)	Scottish Road Weather Line -	(01898) 567 598

PRINTED BY CARNMOR PRINT & DESIGN
95/97 LONDON ROAD, PRESTON, LANCS.